Assignments Matter

ASCD MEMBER BOOK

Many ASCD members received this book as a
member benefit upon its initial release.

Learn more at: **www.ascd.org/memberbooks**

Eleanor Dougherty

Assignments Matter

Making the Connections That Help Students Meet Standards

Alexandria, Virginia USA

1703 N. Beauregard St. • Alexandria, VA 22311-1714 USA
Phone: 800-933-2723 or 703-578-9600 • Fax: 703-575-5400
Website: www.ascd.org • E-mail: member@ascd.org
Author guidelines: www.ascd.org/write

Gene R. Carter, *Executive Director;* Ed Milliken, *Interim Chief Program Development Officer;* Carole Hayward, *Interim Publisher;* Laura Lawson, *Acquisitions Editor;* Julie Houtz, Director, *Book Editing & Production;* Ernesto Yermoli, *Editor;* Georgia Park, *Senior Graphic Designer;* Mike Kalyan, *Production Manager;* Keith Demmons, *Desktop Publishing Specialist;* Kyle Steichen, *Production Specialist*

Printed in the United States of America. Cover art © 2012 by ASCD. ASCD publications present a variety of viewpoints. The views expressed or implied in this book should not be interpreted as official positions of the Association.

All web links in this book are correct as of the publication date below but may have become inactive or otherwise modified since that time. If you notice a deactivated or changed link, please e-mail books@ascd.org with the words "Link Update" in the subject line. In your message, please specify the web link, the book title, and the page number on which the link appears.

ASCD Member Book, No. FY12-1 (Sept. 2012, PSI+). ASCD Member Books mail to Premium (P), Select (S), and Institutional Plus (I+) members on this schedule: Jan., PSI+; Feb., P; Apr., PSI+; May, P; July, PSI+; Aug., P; Sept., PSI+; Nov., PSI+; Dec., P. Select membership was formerly known as Comprehensive membership.

PAPERBACK ISBN: 978-1-4166-1440-1
ASCD product #112048

Also available as an e-book (see Books in Print for the ISBNs).
Quantity discounts for the paperback edition only: 10–49 copies, 10%; 50+ copies, 15%; for 1,000 or more copies, call 800-933-2723, ext. 5634, or 703-575-5634. For desk copies: member@ascd.org.

Library of Congress Cataloging-in-Publication Data

Dougherty, Eleanor, 1947- author.
 Assignments matter : making the connections that help students meet standards / Eleanor Dougherty.
    pages cm
 Includes bibliographical references and index.
 ISBN 978-1-4166-1440-1 (pbk. : alk. paper)
 1. Effective teaching. 2. Learning. 3. Education—Aims and objectives. I. Title.
 LB1025.3.D68 2012
 371.102—dc23
                2012018764

22 21 20 19 18 17 16 15 14 13 12   1 2 3 4 5 6 7 8 9 10 11 12

Assignments Matter

Making the Connections That Help Students Meet Standards

◆ ◆ ◆ ◆ ◆

Acknowledgments

Assignments Matter is in many ways a collective work that evolved over the last two decades, during which I have had the opportunity to work with reform-minded educators who continually looked for ways to make teaching and learning possible while holding themselves and other educators to standards of excellence. I would like to take this unique opportunity to thank the following colleagues and benefactors who have contributed to this work at some point in my career in education and offer my gratitude: Sophie Sa of the Panasonic Foundation for supporting my colleagues and me with a grant in the 1980s to redesign a public high school in which assignments became a significant driver in our curriculum design; Kati Haycock of the Education Trust for recognizing that practice is advocacy; Vicki Phillips of the Gates Foundation for her leadership and support over the years in making assignments matter in school, district, and state communities; Carina Wong at the Gates Foundation for her support in taking assignment-making to a new level; my colleagues on the Literacy Design Collaborative team, Marilyn Crawford, Stacy Galiatsos, Lee Kappes, Cathy Feldman, Anne Lewis, Jill Cannamela, Mark Baier, Terry Roberts, and Laura Billings, for transforming assignments into a national strategy; Jennifer Frentress and Guillarme Gendre for urging me on through the writing of this book; and Carlton Jordan for helping me evolve the methods in this book over a decade of assignment-making in classrooms and workshops across the country. There are many others, particularly the teachers and educators who make assignments matter every day in their classroom—thank you.

◆ ◆ ◆ ◆ ◆

Introduction

Assignments Matter evolved over more than a decade of coaching and working with teachers across the country in an effort to make classroom instruction more effective and manageable. It draws on this experience and focuses on teaching literacy practices by employing assignments in the late-elementary through the secondary years.

Teaching that challenges students to meet expectations is hard work. It takes thoughtful planning and skill to deliver instruction effectively. One way teachers can make their work more challenging for students and manageable for themselves is to insert assignments into their coursework.

As described in this book, an assignment is a recipe for teaching and learning. Like a good recipe, an assignment is a written statement specifying a charge and a process for accomplishing something. In the classroom, this "something" is a product that demonstrates learning: an essay, a science exhibit, a debate, a readers theater, or a proposal to the school board. And, like a good recipe, assignments produce results.

Assignments Matter has two aims. The first is to guide educators—teachers and administrators—in the craft of creating quality assignments by articulating a design process that demystifies and streamlines assignment-making, which is often a time-consuming, after-hours project for teachers. The approach outlined in these pages is part procedural and part meta-cognitive, prompting you to think about how and why you are making decisions while you follow the seven steps of assignment-making. The book's second aim is to help educators become more aware of assignments' impact on teaching and learning. Teachers make instructional decisions every minute of the classroom day; assignments make some of those decisions easier and more relevant, which is important because we know that those who teach "in a most deliberate and visible manner" make learning to high expectations possible (Hattie, 2008, p. 23).

As you gain familiarity with assignments, you will find more and varied ways to make assignments matter, using them to set the stage for effective teaching. In doing so, you make learning possible in your classroom every day. The method described in *Assignments Matter* for crafting assignments aligns your teaching to standards and sets up a teaching and learning process involving specific content and skills. When closely aligned to learning goals, assignments are your means for challenging students and providing them with the clarity they need to meet your goals. *Assignments Matter* offers a systematic way to develop assignments and guidance on the thinking involved in the process of crafting them—or as much as is possible with only words to convey a rather fluid process of making choices about what to teach and how.

Assignments Matter is divided into three sections and eight chapters. The first section, "Why and What," provides a rationale in Chapter 1 for regarding assignments as necessary instructional tools, and in Chapter 2 discusses the "basics," including the differences among three types of tasks. The second section, "In the Classroom," is primarily designed for teachers. Chapter 3 guides you through a series of steps for crafting an assignment. As you manage each step, you make decisions about what you want to teach and what you want students to produce as evidence of learning. Chapter 4 discusses instruction, including instructional *touchstones*, four classic strategies that work with any assignment. Chapter 5 describes a strategy for sequencing assignments in units, projects, and courses; doing so creates a curriculum grounded in assignments. The third section, "Beyond the Classroom," is designed, in general, for coaches, curriculum designers, and administrators. Chapter 6 describes a school or districtwide strategy called "Anchor" assignments, which are common assignments taught across a grade or a department to create collaboration, consensus, and continuity within a professional community. Chapter 7 discusses ways in which you can design schedules and staffing arrangements to create instructional environments that make it possible to teach assignments effectively. Finally, Chapter 8 discusses how to create data and feedback from assignments and student work to help you decide next steps and other supports.

◆ ◆ ◆ ◆ ◆

Part 1

Why and What

This section opens with an explanation of the rationale behind assignments and continues with a description of the basic elements of assignments: prompts, rubrics, and products.

1

Why Assignments Matter

I want to be as emphatic as possible: the impact of the actual,
taught curriculum on school quality, on student learning, is
indescribably important.

—Schmoker, 2006, p. 36

When considering the prospect of creating assignments, some people might ask, "Why bother?" Ruth Mitchell, who designed a protocol for analyzing tasks in her book *Front-End Alignment* (1996), has a good answer to this question and is well known by her colleagues for saying, "Students can do no better than the assignments they are given." Just any assignment admittedly will not improve achievement, but well-crafted assignments hold the potential to make learning and teaching more focused and relevant because in the crafting process teachers must be deliberate and highly aware of the context, content, and charge involved in an assignment. Implementing well-crafted assignments is worth the effort. Indeed, my work with colleagues over the years in educational settings, including schools, districts, and states, suggests that assignments may well be the missing link in school reform efforts to improve student achievement.

Effects on Student Performance

More than a decade ago, I cowrote an article that discussed the lack of challenging tasks in classrooms and the impact that deficiency has on student performance, and how, unfortunately, this pattern of weak tasks without content and clear purpose continues (Barth & Dougherty, 1997). Too many students, my colleagues and I observed, spent classroom time on activities, such as filling in worksheets, coloring maps, underlining textbook chapters, and listening to computer-activated lessons and read-alouds. In these settings, students were engaged in tasks with little relevant content, and often teachers could not tell us why they were teaching these tasks or what was actually at work in the tasks. For example, a task we saw repeatedly asked students to create book covers, an activity I still see today at all grade levels (although its cousin, the poster, may be more prevalent). As teachers analyzed what was learned and taught in this task, it became clear that the task asked students to spend more time on creating borders and lettering for their covers than on analyzing the themes and characters in the book. By using Mitchell's protocol involving a process of analysis called *Standards in Practice*, the teachers were able to understand that their tasks were unaligned to standards and did not help students learn the topics, issues, and questions embedded in a rigorous curriculum (Education Trust, 2006; Mitchell, 1996).

The Link Between Expectations and Achievement

According to Robert Marzano, "High expectations and pressure to achieve refer to establishing *challenging goals* for students" (2003, p. 35). The reverse is also true, in that low expectations and little pressure to achieve cause poor achievement. When teachers present students with low-rigor tasks, they create low achievement even when students do well on these tasks. In addition, such tasks contribute to the boredom students so often complain about when they spend too many hours on work that is routine and bland, often centered on discrete skills. In these situations, students miss opportunities to acquire basic skills in an intellectual environment that would allow them to apply those skills. When students perform low-rigor tasks, they are unsure of why they are doing them and how they will benefit, even if standards are posted on the wall. Such teaching results in damaging experiences for struggling students as well as their more skilled peers. According to national and international data, even strong students aren't progressing as much as they can or should (Education Trust, 2008). If, on the other hand, assignments are taught with high expectations and pressure to achieve, then students gain the knowledge and skills they need to take on a wide range of environments and opportunities.

The Importance of Explicit Teaching

When assignments are not taught or are not taught explicitly, students lose out on the academic and intellectual experiences that assignments offer. According to Harvard researchers who have studied classroom dynamics, the "task predicts performance" (City, Elmore, Fieman, & Teitel, 2009, p. 30). If assignments are not of high quality and are not relevant to the curriculum, then learning will also be of low quality and loosely connected to the curriculum, if at all. Teaching and learning constitute a reciprocal process. Ineffective instruction is often distinguished by a loosely regulated plan, and students spend classroom time going through the motions of learning but not producing solid evidence of that learning. In these classrooms, the purpose for doing activities is lost, and learning loses energy and meaning. To coin a phrase, a lesson without an assignment is a lot like a carriage with no horse and no place to go. In contrast, a well-crafted assignment ensures that instruction will provide students with a goal and the power to get there, enabling them to engage in rigorous and interesting academic contexts as they acquire the content and skills necessary to participate in academic coursework. Most important, assignments create teaching and learning opportunities to think and learn about ideas, topics, events, and questions—about specific content in the curriculum. This is why a quality assignment is the hallmark of effective instruction.

Ms. H.'s classroom is an example of intentional teaching with assignments playing an important role. Ms. H. is a middle school English teacher who employs assignments to teach specific content and skills. In this example, she asked students to recommend a book to their peers, an assignment aligned to the Common Core State Standards (CCSS) for English Language Arts (ELA) (the standards are discussed at length in the next section of this chapter). Her purpose was to teach students how to write a critical book review, which is an assignment built around skills of critical thinking and argumentation. On the surface this seems to be a simple enough task, and in another classroom it may well have been given as homework, with very little direct teaching. As a result, students typically produce a long paragraph retelling parts of the book they liked but not producing a critical review.

In contrast, Ms. H. used a template from the Literacy Design Collaborative (or LDC, an effort funded by the Gates Foundation in 2009–11 to develop a national literacy strategy) to develop the following prompt:

> Would you recommend *Green Angel*, a novel, to your peers?
> After reading and analyzing this modern-day fairy tale, write
> a critical review in which you address the question. Support
> your review with evidence from the book.

She then taught the students, step by step, the skills and strategies they needed to employ to produce a critical review. The result was that students learned the difference between retelling and a critical review: how to make a claim and support it with a set of reasons based on the genre and elements of fiction. Their work was consistently well developed and well expressed. Having learned how to construct a basic argumentative essay in the language of the discipline, these students were positioned to take on even more challenging prompts.

Ms. H.'s thoughtful instruction more than suggests that the value of assignments as a way to manage and deliver instruction serves both teachers and students. Somewhere we got sidetracked away from this classic way of teaching, and in many classrooms it is hard to find assignments as defined in this book, except in advanced placement (AP), International Baccalaureate (IB), and some honors courses. That leaves thousands of students without the benefit of assignments. Instead instruction is typically focused around activities, programs, textbooks, workbooks, and homework. In such low-demand settings, students tend to do one thing at a time—a worksheet on Monday, a spelling test on Friday—rather than accomplish a cycle of learning in which they apply skills and content.

A simple calibration exercise helped my colleagues and me provide data to show staff what, in fact, everyday instruction was composed of and that assignments were not commonly employed in classrooms. One particularly revealing calibration showed a middle school staff that only one task out of more than a hundred could be classified as an assignment—a science lab report. The vast majority of this sample of tasks consisted of worksheets; many involved grammar, computation, spelling, and elementary wordplay skills and were clearly unaligned to middle school standards. These data provided at least part of the explanation for this school's struggle to improve achievement.

Like these surveys, a DataWorks calibration analysis of tasks gathered in California similarly showed that tasks are too often unaligned. In their analysis, only half of 5th grade tasks were aligned to standards, and alignment decreased in higher grades (Fiello, 2005). This is sobering news.

It is not a stretch to predict that low-rigor instructional experiences produce weak outcomes and the achievement gaps we are witnessing in the performance data (Education Trust, 2008). If students spend their school day repeating, retelling, writing paragraphs, and filling in blanks rather than applying those skills to explore interesting questions and issues or to solve problems, they won't achieve to new levels. The good news is that teaching that produces low achievement can be changed. Following Richard Elmore's commonsense advice, you can change the task to produce better results since the "task predicts performance" (2010, p. 4). Assignments, well crafted and well taught, can help you and your students make that transformation.

The Common Core State Standards for ELA

In the current educational environment, the emergence of the Common Core State Standards for English Language Arts and Literacy in History/Social Studies, Science, and Technical Subjects and their equivalent in mathematics represent new educational terrain for teachers and students. The CCSS differ from the last decade's standards in that they are contextualized and compact, and they emphasize the role of literacy in all core subjects. These standards cannot be taught superficially; they are not long lists of discrete skills, to be checked off in a lesson plan or assessed only on quizzes. They demand that students acquire academic skills that they apply across the disciplines, particularly those involving analyses of ideas and texts, reading a range of texts of sufficient complexity, and writing in response to reading (Conley, 2011). Students will also need to apply other literacy skills in language usage, speaking, and listening to support and enhance their abilities to communicate what is learned. As well, students will need to acquire cognitive skills in logic and reasoning as readers, speakers, and writers. The work for teachers, then, is to transform the CCSS into practices that enable students to become literate, independent, and critical thinkers. The draft frameworks for two CCSS assessments—one from the Partnership for Assessment of Readiness for College and Careers (PARCC; available at www.parcconline .org) and the other from the SMARTER Balanced Assessment Consortium (SBAC; available at www.k12.wa.us/SMARTER/)—reinforce these academic skills.

A report written by David T. Conley, who has long researched the alignment between high school and college curriculums, emphasizes the role of college readiness in implementing curriculum, stating, "These standards are not geared to what should or does occur in high schools as much as to what will be expected of students in college" (2011, p. 7). In addition, in his book *College Knowledge*, Conley (2005) has documented the frequency and types of papers and the amount of reading that college coursework requires. Papers of 5 to 10 pages were common, as was reading more than 10 texts. High-performing students read and wrote almost twice as much as the national average.

Assignments are excellent vehicles to prepare students for the routines and demands of college work. High school students who learn how to write arguments in response to reading, for example, will clearly be better prepared than those who fill out worksheets or produce cut-and-paste research papers. In the process they can build a strong grade point average that is academically meaningful. A grade point average is a strong predictor—better than scores on admissions exams—of first-year success in college coursework (Noble & Sawyer, 2004). That is, coursework consisting of assignments aligned to college readiness—in which students are prepared for the volume of reading, essays, and reports they will have to do in college—makes their high school years even more beneficial (ACT, 2006).

By crafting assignments with close attention to alignment to the CCSS and to your own state standards, you and your colleagues in the core disciplines can help students become high achievers and be ready for college or careers. As a middle school teacher whom I worked with stated, "My students are doing better and more challenging work since I started giving assignments." To align your assignments with the CCSS, you and your colleagues should strive to do the following:

- Teach literacy skills in all content areas.
- Teach students to comprehend and critique a variety of texts and ideas.
- Write prompts that ask students to write or orally explain in response to reading.
- Include speaking and listening as a means of comprehending and communicating.
- Expect that students will use and write language to communicate appropriately for an audience and a purpose.
- Require evidence from texts and credible sources.
- Create opportunities for students to use and manage technology to learn and produce their own products.
- Write instructional plans that document and plot the teaching that transforms an assignment into learning.

Reflection Activity: Compare the "old" standard to the CCSS for 8th grade. How do their expectations for learning differ?
- *Old standard:* By the end of the 8th grade, students will identify the main idea and supporting details in what they have read.
- *CCSS standard:* Determine a theme or central idea of a text and analyze its development over the course of the text, including its relationship to the characters, setting, and plot; provide an objective summary of the text.

Making Assignments Matter

Aligning your assignments with the CCSS and state standards is certainly a major step in making assignments matter. But in addition to the benefits of alignment, assignments, along with instructional plans, also matter because they document teaching and learning, providing tangible feedback for both teachers and students about learning at different stages of the instructional cycle. Assignments engage students in purposeful work each day of the cycle, from introduction of a prompt to production of a product. You can test all you want or engage in entertaining activities, but students learn when goals are clear and relevant and they are challenged to think. Assignments are a vehicle to do just that.

By inserting assignments into a teaching routine, you can take an immediate step to heed Elmore's advice, noted earlier, to "change the task." A switch from a long sequence of *activities*, such as worksheets and other one-dimensional tasks, to well-crafted and well-taught *assignments* ups the challenge for heftier performances as prescribed in the prompt, the rubric, and the product (each of which is discussed in detail in the following chapters). This seemingly simple switch to assignments causes a ripple effect that not only changes the kinds of tasks students engage in but also changes the larger curriculum by creating a higher degree of coherence. Unlike teaching that consists of a series of activities, an assignment involves a cycle of learning, in which students progress through a sequence of steps that lead to a product. This product is evidence of learning constructed around a specific purpose and context—writing an essay to compare government policies or building a scale model for a local shelter, for example. In this way, assignments activate the research and practice theories on effective instruction. During one of our LDC sessions, a group of teachers new to assignment-making admitted that their early assignments "weren't that good." Nevertheless, they reported to researchers who monitored the project that students still performed better and showed a higher degree of involvement than in the past (Research for Action, 2011).

Artifacts of Teaching

Assignments by their nature provide outputs in the form of products and documented instruction; they are necessary artifacts of effective teaching, and, as a report by a national organization states, "Effectiveness is best defined as the practical outputs of teaching" (Jupp, 2009, p. 1). Well-taught assignments as outputs of teaching matter not only in the classroom but also in the broader view of the profession because assignments help teachers improve their practice and aim to do what effective teaching also aims to do—succeed in teaching students what they need to know and be able to do. Madeleine Hunter (1993) gave us her now classic list of criteria that define effective teaching, and it includes the same features found in assignments: alignment to standards, focused instruction, guided practice, and closure. Laura Goe (2009), a researcher who has studied teacher performance models for the National Comprehensive Center for Teacher Quality, recommends the inclusion of assignments in teacher performance reviews. This recommendation makes sense because assignments are *evidence* of outcomes as well as the production of outcomes.

To meet expectations for effectiveness, a teacher makes many decisions, deciding what to teach and which strategies, methods, and resources—whatever it takes—will best guide learning until students acquire targeted skills and internalize content. Charlotte Danielson has observed that "a teacher makes over 3,000 nontrivial decisions daily" (1996, p. 2). Assignment-making can assist teachers in making these decisions and developing coursework that systematically provides outputs to demonstrate effectiveness. Unlike assessments, which provide documentation *after* instruction, assignments evidence how well teachers make instructional decisions and choices in the teaching moment. Because teachers have control over the inputs in an assignment and the process of teaching them, they can manage instruction and pacing to ensure better outcomes.

Despite their importance and usefulness in the educational environment, assignments have not been studied historically as artifacts of classroom teaching. Instead, educators have tended to focus on instructional strategies as stand-alone practices. Had there been more research, we might have a better understanding of the dynamics of assignments. Current initiatives focused on tasks and undertaken by the Gates Foundation and other educational organizations should help inform what types, formats, and resources best shape effective assignment-making and teaching. Nevertheless, a link between assignments and effective teaching seems apparent if for no other reason than the fact that an assignment involves what effective teachers do—engaging students in complex thinking and skills using appropriate and focused instruction.

Support for Three Principles of Effective Instruction

The work of researchers over the years suggests three principles of effective instruction, all of which are supported by assignment-making.

1. Effective instruction is clear about what to teach and how (Danielson, 1996; Hunter, 1993; Marzano, 2007). Assignment-making requires teachers to clarify what to teach and how to teach it. It is the assignment continuum, from the introduction of a prompt through instruction to product delivery and scoring, that propels teaching, resulting in demonstrated learning. Teachers strive to answer questions about purpose and relevancy: "Why am I teaching . . . ?" "Is this a significant concept in the subject curriculum?"

Common sense suggests that teaching cannot be focused and purposeful without clarity about goals. You must know why you are teaching an assignment and where that assignment fits into the larger curriculum. Teaching that wanders from one strategy to another does not improve student performance. As well, tasks that are too complex and carry an overload of cognitive demands are equally confusing and hard to manage (Stein, Brown, & Forman, 1996). In contrast, a well-crafted assignment takes into account what students can handle, while simultaneously stretching them. It clearly states the immediate goal and articulates the challenge in terms students can understand. It tells students what to do and how well to do it. Assignments are also aligned to long-term goals, whether those goals are building toward proficiency on assessments or college and workplace readiness.

Jeanne Chall's (2000) study of elementary curriculum and instruction also reinforces what educators know: that clear, purposeful teaching produces the best results for students. Assignments are a vehicle for doing just that. Teachers who are purposeful about their teaching know the whys and wherefores of their instructional choices, and they employ an array of practices and strategies to manage the teaching process. Such teaching results in students gaining deeper understanding of content and application of skills because the teaching interacts with, intercepts, and guides the learning process at the right places and the right moments.

2. Effective teaching is formative, providing feedback that allows teachers to adjust their instruction and scaffold learning (Reeves, 2006; Stiggins, Aster, Chappius, & Chappius, 2006). Assignments provide clear evidence of what is taught and what is learned in response to instruction because both teacher work and student work are documented. My colleagues and I found that a task—sometimes an assignment, sometimes not—accompanied by a class set of papers tells a lot about the effectiveness of instruction because a class set reveals what was taught and what wasn't taught in the classroom. If, for example, we analyzed a class set of papers in which each paper demonstrated a pattern of thought, we knew that all students were taught how to organize their thoughts in writing, even if some managed it more successfully than others. The opposite was also the case: a class set in which students wrote in long sprawling paragraphs lacking a pattern of thought indicated they weren't taught organizational patterns.

Recent practice theory and research are looking at tasks as the best indicators of what is taught in the classroom and what is learned. Harvard researchers identify tasks as the central dynamic of the instructional core (City et al., 2009). They include tasks in their six principles as predictors of performance and evidence of learning that make for an authentic accountability system.

3. Effective teaching sets high expectations. When assignments are aligned to high expectations, students are challenged no matter what skill sets or content background they bring into courses. The Education Trust, a nonprofit that advocates for students in public schools, similarly found that "high-impact schools have consistently higher expectations for all students, regardless of students' prior academic performance" (2005, p. 4). The structure of an assignment and the process detailed in the following chapters help ensure that the work students engage in is aligned to content and skill standards. As you move through the seven steps for crafting an assignment you will identify the standards to inform the content of your prompt and rubric.

Think of a well-crafted assignment in the same way you think about a well-crafted pitcher: both must have a sense of harmony while doing the work they are meant to do. That is, a beautiful pitcher must also pour without spilling over in the wrong places. When you make an assignment matter, you have made it functional and worthwhile in time, effort, and achievement.

In Chapter 2 you will find further discussions of the distinctions among three types of tasks: assignments, assessments, and activities. It's important to make these distinctions, to avoid confusion about the purposes behind each type and how each plays a role in teaching. You will be drawing on your understanding of these differences as you craft and teach your assignment.

◆ ◆ ◆ ◆ ◆

2

The Basics

An assignment differs from other tasks because it consists of a prompt, a rubric, and a product, which together set a clear purpose and process for engaging in academic work. An instructional plan supports and delivers the assignment. Assignments, unlike assessments or activities, are intentionally *taught*. They are not merely given, as in "I gave an assignment," or assigned as homework for someone else to teach or for students to figure out themselves. Instead, when well crafted, assignments become centerpieces for demanding and interesting learning experiences. Even more powerful than a single assignment is a series of assignments. If students engage in connected assignments, they acquire the content and skills that allow them to progress over the year and from course to course with confidence. Schools and districts that teach together, collaborating on one or more common assignments, build consensus and collaboration in ways that self-contained teaching cannot.

Assignments stimulate students' thinking around ideas and questions that demand careful examination. They can involve students in creating traditional products, such as written essays and reports, as well as products using video, digital media, and combinations of both.

If you look around, and listen, potential assignments are everywhere. During a conversation someone might say, for example, that she "wonders about" how or why or what or where, as in "How does Wi-Fi work?" or "Why is the sea green?" or "What is the ratio of emissions to clean air in our town?" or "Why do saguaro cacti grow only in one area of the country?" Browsing at the local stores, you find pamphlets and flyers with lists of topics in the sciences, construction math, and many other subjects. Every page of a newspaper or magazine provides fodder for assignments in headlines and articles. You don't need to search long for the "stuff" of assignments because the questions, topics, content, and issues that make up assignments are in front of you every day. Here's an example of a prompt starter taken from a *New York Times* headline: "Do you have free will? Yes, it's the only choice."

The Architecture of Assignments

The architecture of an assignment promotes thinking about content. According to Briars (2011), an assignment is a kind of task that influences "learners by directing their attention to particular aspects of content and by specifying ways to process information." You craft an assignment by placing it on three pillars: a prompt, a rubric, and a product. The *prompt* challenges students to explore content in some way, using skills to produce evidence of learning. An effective prompt sets the stage for thinking about something. Some assignments may even provoke students to see others and ideas differently. The *rubric* describes the expectations for a response to the prompt. The *product* demonstrates learning as both a process and tangible evidence. Together these three features of an assignment support teaching and learning.

In the following assignment, students learn details about a critical Civil War battle to help them understand the role of strategy and geography in military outcomes, a theme they can apply to the study of other battles in history and current events. The evidence of learning is their product, the annotated time line. There are many ways to write a rubric, as you will see in the next chapter, but whatever method you use, a classroom rubric is ultimately a communication tool to help students understand the qualities they should strive for in their work, or what Lynn Sharratt and Michael Fullan (2012) call "success criteria."

> *Prompt:* Design a detailed annotated time line that shows events and circumstances during the battle at Gettysburg leading to the Union's defeat of the Confederate army.

Rubric: Your time line should include at least 10 time points; annotations must be accurate and relate one decisive event for each point on your time line.

The architecture of an assignment involves a distinct structure in order to set the stage for a cycle of instruction that moves from an introductory phase, through a period of production, and ends with a completed product. During that cycle, both teachers and students are working: students engage in learning content and skills and ultimately demonstrate that learning in their products; teachers teach students how to do that. An assignment might ask students to read a complex text and explain the author's intent or to question an "urban myth" or to apply science to everyday routines, to name a few possibilities among many. A well-crafted assignment sets up the conditions for teaching as well as learning, detailed in an instructional plan as a coherent learning cycle. During the assignment cycle, students are taught how to engage in and execute a set of demands and produce a product—a composition, an exhibit, a lab report, a speech. The more you craft assignments, the more you will understand the architecture and the dynamic of the cycle.

Assignments in Sequence

Assignments linked together in a series make for powerful coursework. By sequencing assignments, you can build a thematic unit, a project, or a course. Linked assignments create a learning progression in which you control how you increase challenges over time. Each assignment in a series sets the stage for the next one, allowing you to ratchet up complexity and challenge. For example, two or three assignments might make up a community report on an environmental problem or be sequenced in a unit on the United Nations. When you build a series of assignments, you create a staircase effect in which students progress as they acquire skills in successive assignments rather than attempting to handle a long, complex assignment all at once. When you plot this sequence over a term or a year, you create a highly connected and doable curriculum sequence in the process.

Admittedly, crafting and delivering assignments can be time-consuming and demanding for both students and teachers. If you decide to make assignments integral to your curriculum, you will need to create temporal and physical environments that make teaching assignments possible. Teachers need time and space to craft assignments, to teach them, and to score them. Most important, they need time and space to think, individually and collectively, because assignments take their power from teacher knowledge and thinking. To craft a quality assignment involves the skillful confluence of content and pedagogy. Chapter 7 suggests ways to create such environments, because time, space, and resources must be in place to support a curriculum that values assignments.

Assignment, Activity, or Assessment?

Not all tasks are created equal, and different tasks will provoke different levels and kinds of student thinking.
—Stein, Smith, Henningsen, & Silver, 2000, p. 3

Assignments, activities, and assessments are instruments of a teaching experience, but they differ in form and function, and each one plays its unique role. It's important to distinguish among them to clarify what your purposes are. Once you understand these distinctions, you are better able to design and manage crafting assignments either as stand-alone instructional instruments or as a connected series in a unit or a curriculum.

Education jargon is rife with language that we use loosely in a variety of contexts, and one such term that causes confusion is *lesson*. In teacher texts and online sites, a lesson comes in many guises. It might be a series of activities—for example, a visit to a museum or an examination of plant leaves. However, it's rare that these lessons are synonymous with this book's definition of *assignment*. Another term educators use loosely is *assessment*. The current trend is to call any classroom task that we grade or score an assessment, but doing so can blur the distinction between teaching and testing. *Assignment* may be an old-fashioned term, but it is useful here because it conveys specific functions and characteristics, distinct from *activity* and *assessment*. You have already read some discussion about these terms, but they are central to this work, so it's worth revisiting them in more depth.

Assignment—The "ing" in "Teaching"

An assignment involves a task that is taught with a focus on the "ing" in teaching. Assignments are recipes for instructional events—lessons in the best sense—and their main function is to create a context for teaching new content and skills and practicing learned ones. That is, assignments aim to teach for *learning*—not *testing*, as in an assessment, or merely *doing*, as in an activity. The must-have features of an assignment are the following:

- A *prompt* that sets up a charge to do something
- A *product* or performance that demonstrates progress in learning
- A *rubric* that describes how well students need to demonstrate progress

Each feature of an assignment has a function and helps to set teaching in motion and end with closure. The prompt tells students what to do, involving skills, content, and thinking. The product tells them in what form, and the rubric details your expectations for that product. The instructional plan makes sure the assignment is taught.

A sample prompt for 6th graders, from the National Paideia Center/ Literacy Design Collaborative, starts with an essential question:

> What is the proper role of the individual in response to a disaster? After reading passages from the Dalai Lama, John Donne, Marcus Aurelius, and William Stafford on individual responsibility, write a letter to a younger student that addresses the question and supports your position with evidence from the texts.

Prompts can be this challenging or more straightforward, but in either case, an assignment creates a context for learning and thinking.

To ensure students understand not only what they should do but how well they should do it, teachers accompany a prompt with a rubric. Rubrics are scoring guides; some are as simple as a short paragraph or a list, and others, such as rubrics for state assessments, indicate various levels of accomplishment. In some cases, teachers may choose to adjust borrowed rubrics to fit their prompt. In Chapter 3, you will learn how rubric formats and terminology help students understand expectations for products created for assignments.

Before you begin teaching an assignment, you make an *instructional plan*, which spells out step by step, period by period, how the assignment is taught. Your plan takes its cue from your assignment's prompt and rubric because you must teach what you asked students to do. Also, you must teach the rubric's criteria that you will use in scoring their work. Your plan should also pace your assignment and identify intermediate steps that students should take to complete the assignment. Chapter 4 describes instructional strategies that work with any assignment, and Chapter 5 provides a prototype plan for pacing your assignment.

You can save time by borrowing assignment prompts and sometimes instructional plans from credible sources or revising them to fit your purposes. You may have to adjust them to fit your purposes and to align them to standards, but they can provide a starting point. Release items from state assessments, for example, can be good sources for prompts. Appendix D provides some sample prompts from various sources. One warning: Beware of lessons that may look like an assignment but consist of only a long list of activities, sometimes with an "assessment" tacked on the end. Such lessons are not assignments because they lack the components that make an assignment complete and functional. A typical example is a middle school science lesson from an online source that consists of four pages of standards, activities, and topics. In this example, there is a disconnect between the heft of the task and what students are asked to do, which is a simple activity unaligned to the rigor of the long list of standards and related activities. The activity is short, sweet, and unaligned: "Create a set of vocabulary cards with hand-drawn pictures of animal words." Clearly, a steady dose of such tasks not only causes students to tune out but also causes teaching to lose its impact. In such a classroom, activities are checked off and teaching moves on, leaving some students confused or apathetic. Furthermore, teaching this way poses long-lasting problems for students because if "lessons" involve only a series of activities—ditto sheets, reading circles, jigsaws, graphic organizers, underlining textbook chapters, or making book covers—students cannot learn to the depth of understanding necessary to do well on a follow-up assessment. These tasks cannot claim to be aligned to standards, so they are a waste of instructional time for both teachers and students. An important function of assignments involves alignment not only to standards but also to assessments, particularly end-of-unit or -term assessments, so that students are prepared and confident in testing situations. Most of us who have braved several years of schooling have experienced a teacher who lectured, put students in reading circles, and assigned graphic organizers, projects, and seminars. But when you got the test, it didn't look anything like what you did in class. "Not fair!" you said.

A new teacher related how he figured out that instruction should be closely tied to what students encounter when they are assessed or when they have to perform. Analyzing the AP results from his first year of teaching, he saw that only one student had passed. He realized that he had spent so much time on content that he had not given students opportunities to learn how to use that content in a written essay, which is what they had to do to pass the AP exam. The next year he gave a short assignment requiring a brief essay each week, focusing each time on a small set of skills that students needed so they could achieve a score of 3 or better on the AP scale. He wasn't able to come to school the day his students took the exam, but the substitute reported to him that she had never seen a class so comfortable with an exam. Every student settled into the writing task and seemed unruffled, she told him. He was even more pleased when he got the results. Most of his students passed, and two got 5s.

Reflection Activity: How often do you give assignments, as defined in this chapter, during a term, semester, or year? Take a moment to reflect on how assignments might motivate students to engage in your curriculum.

Activity—The "ing" in "Learning"

Activities are instructional strategies and practices that teachers employ to help students acquire new content and skills and to practice old ones. Activities are not scored. They are a means to an end, and they are most powerful when they are set in the contexts of assignments.

Activities *serve* assignments and are specifically chosen to teach students how to do something (a skill) or to know something (content). To instruct students in the specific content and skills embedded in an assignment, teachers teach—they guide, model, demonstrate, lecture, lead field trips, or bring in experts. They do whatever it takes to ensure students learn an assignment's content and skills sufficiently to move on to another learning cycle. For example, creating a value line is an activity that can help students to understand that people have a range of opinions about free speech and to shape their own claim in preparation for, say, a debate. Alone, without the context of an assignment, making a value line is fun to do but unfettered academically.

Volumes have been written on instructional activities, and Chapter 4 highlights a few that work with any assignment. All teachers employ activities because that is how teaching ignites learners' interest, stimulates their understanding, and helps them learn how to perform a skill or see how something works. However, no matter how good these activities are, they are weak or ineffective on their own because doing something without a context is like being in a boat without a rudder, leaving students in the moment rather than progressing down a path toward a goal. Take, for example, reading aloud, a frequently used practice. Just reading aloud doesn't help students much unless the activity is set in the context of a specific act of communicating. For example, if reading aloud is integrated into an assignment that asks for students to participate in a readers theater for parent night, then reading with a strong, clear, fluid voice makes sense and has consequences, most likely applause. When you craft an assignment, you will eventually decide which activities best support the learner in the process of acquiring content and skills embedded in that assignment.

Once you have written a prompt and a rubric, you have crafted your assignment. You will write an instructional plan to plot how to deliver the assignment to include the sequence of instructional events that transform the assignment into learning. These are the strategies, activities, and tools you will use to ensure students learn the content and skills embedded in the assignment. Because the assignment is aligned to standards, you also transform standards into practice, ensuring that students not only learn grade-level curriculum but are prepared for next-level coursework. Because an assignment creates contexts for learning and is constructed to determine what students do and how well they do it, crafting assignments is critical professional work in which teachers determine what is taught and what is learned each day.

Reflection Activity: What activities would you employ to help students acquire the following skills? For example, students could engage in rhythm games to learn multiplication tables.

- Read closely
- Draw conclusions
- Apply grammatical rules
- Follow lab procedures
- Do research on the Web
- Use topographical maps
- Read statistical information
- Participate in a discussion

Assessments—Evidence of Learning

The term *assessment* appears frequently in the education lexicon, so the distinction between *assessment* and *assignment* deserves an explanation here. Assessments are distinct from assignments in that they are *not* taught. They may look like assignments, but they are used for different purposes: to evaluate student progress toward learning specific content and skills taught in the classroom. Assessments are necessary components of a course because they give feedback on student learning in order to inform teachers about student progress and the effectiveness of instructional choices. This feedback allows teachers to "change the task" to create better opportunities for learning.

In the educational lexicon, assignments are often referred to as "formative tasks." However, I prefer to make the distinction to ensure that teachers understand and act on the fact that assignments are taught, explicitly and intentionally. Classroom summative assessments are tests or exams teachers assign to help them assess the degree to which students can apply a set of content and skills independently.

Admittedly, assignments could be called formative assessments. According to a national group that monitors assessments, formative assessment "occurs when teachers feed information back to students in ways that enable students to learn better, or when students engage in a similar, self-reflective process" (Fairtest, 2007). Also, the assignments included in this book can be considered formative assessments because the learning during an assignment is a "self-reflective process" meant to increase student understanding and skill. As well, the teacher gains understanding of student learning needs and can adjust instruction as students work through an assignment.

If you choose to call assignments "formative assessments," here's a caution: When educators refer to all tasks as "assessments," experience has taught me that some teachers tend to emphasize coverage over learning. The term *assessment* connotes testing, and this implies that teachers shouldn't "really teach," as one veteran science teacher admitted. She thought that the depth and intentionality of instruction I was talking about was "cheating." As a result of such conversations, in this book I choose to use the term *assignment* to emphasize that these tasks are taught and to give educators relief from the assessment-ridden language of the current education lexicon. Just remember, quality assignments are the hallmark of effective teaching; teaching made up mostly of testing does not improve student learning.

Reflection Activity: Discuss how you assess student learning in your classrooms. How do you use assignments and assessments as feedback? How do you use the feedback? What other ways do you monitor student progress? Can you cite a time when you "changed the task" based on feedback?

What Is Rigor? Demands and Qualities

There are two more elements necessary to crafting assignments, and they make all the difference between effective and ineffective instruction. Teachers have often asked me, "What is rigor?" That's a good question, because students improve and progress when curriculum is rigorous. Yet educators and policymakers use the term *rigorous* so often that it is rarely understood by two or more people as the same thing. In an attempt to bring clarity and allow for a more analytical discussion about rigorous instruction, I refer in this book to two features of an assignment that constitute rigor: *demands* and *qualities*. Each term describes expectations for student work that must be present for an assignment to be deemed rigorous.

Demands and qualities are conveyed through the combined content in a prompt and a rubric. *Demands* constitute the "do it this way" element and are usually described in the prompt as well as the rubric. *Qualities* are those characteristics that distinguish student work that is poorly or marginally executed from work that is well performed as measured against expectations set out in a rubric for proficient or advanced levels. It is the "how good is good enough and more" element. Demands and qualities take their cue from standards and other sources that articulate academic learning goals. If you want to see workplace or authentic learning goals, look at classified ads or position descriptions; you will find language that describes real-world demands and qualities of performance. "Good communication skills" is an example of a job-ad skill that students use in school as well as in the workplace. (The Partnership for 21st Century Skills has developed curriculum maps that consist of authentic and work-related skills and are used by many states. Go to www.21stcenturyskills.org.)

Think of demands as descriptors that set conditions and establish a level of difficulty by complicating the task and asking students to manage a number of elements. To respond to a prompt that says, "Write an 800-word analysis of NAFTA," students would have to know how to select and sort through resources, determine and analyze the elements of NAFTA, draw a conclusion, and write a report to specifications.

Qualities, on the other hand, express how well students should perform as demonstrated in their work. Terms such as *accurate, logical, insightful,* and *convincing* describe qualities found in student products. By adding quality-related language, such as *convincing,* the NAFTA prompt takes on another dimension and purpose: "Write an 800-word analysis of NAFTA that aims to convince local workers to support it." When you write the rubric, you further clarify qualities by using language that partners with demands: "Students produce a *convincing* speech that provides *relevant* supports and examples."

When writing a prompt, watch out for pitfalls that keep assignment demands misaligned to standards. One such pitfall is low-rigor content or skills. Another is demands that are developmentally inappropriate. This misalignment happens when an assignment in middle school asks students to do what they did in elementary school—for example, a book report that asks students to retell rather than analyze. By middle school, students should be analyzing a character, theme, or some other aspect of literature. A similar pitfall occurs when an assignment's rubric asks for demands but not qualities, resulting in a to-do list without reference to qualities. Such a list neglects to communicate to students, as well as words can, the difference between passing and not passing. A suggestion in Chapter 3 is that rubrics be accompanied by model student or professional products as often as possible to more fully help students understand the goal of their own work.

A middle school student gave me this example. He was asked in his middle school social studies class to draw a poster for a unit on Egypt. The academic standard that addresses Egypt calls for students to be able to explain the major contributions of the Egyptian civilization. However, he was not given an assignment—there was no prompt, no rubric—just some directions on how to make a poster. He didn't have to muster up anything more than a "pretty picture" (his words). As a result of this task, he and his peers engaged in little thought, although they devoted some evening time on several unrelated demands—drawing and neatness—with only superficial attention to the standard. He assumed that to "pass" he would have to have something about Egypt on his poster, be neat, and use lots of color. Such a task begs us to ask, "Is this a social studies assignment or an art assignment? Is this worth doing?" His comment was that it was "a waste of my time."

He knew a lot about Egypt because he had parents who nurtured his knowledge base, discussing Egypt over the dinner table. Many students may not have this out-of-school advantage, and they lose out in at least two ways. First, they do not acquire content that allows them to make connections as they study other civilizations in future grades. Second, they do not learn to research or to "integrate information" as stated in the Common Core State Standards. When assignments are aligned to low-level demands and superficial qualities, students learn little that is relevant to the curriculum or the assessment system. The continual use of low-demand assignments—or no assignments at all—is the day-to-day cause of low student achievement. Consequently, the benefits of high-demand, quality assignments and instruction cannot be overestimated (Reeves, 2006; Schmoker, 2011).

By adjusting demands and qualities in assignments, teachers establish control over the pace and effort involved in the student learning process. (Chapter 5 discusses in detail how to moderate demands and qualities to pace a sequence so that students receive progressively more challenging assignments.) This is not to say that teachers should never employ easier assignments. However, an easier assignment doesn't mean a 2nd grade task in middle school. Easier means, for example, reading a less challenging text, but one that still offers room to think, or laugh, or reflect. Sometimes it's good practice to take a breather, especially when students have worked on a demanding assignment. Giving students an easier assignment can also be useful for introducing a new skill or content, for allowing students who didn't "get it" the first time to try again, or for reinforcing some aspect of a more complex set of skills. Like the artisan who sometimes uses simple techniques and at other times more elaborate ones to produce an effect, teachers may need to adjust expectations in a scaffolded way so that they challenge students from easier to harder or lower to higher levels of performance. The important point is that teaching that never raises expectations will not raise student achievement. Techniques for varying demands by adjusting length and complexity are discussed in Chapter 5.

Reflection Activity: Consider each of the following prompts by analyzing the (1) content and skills involved in each and (2) demands and qualities. What makes one prompt more demanding than the other? What qualities would you expect to see in the student work for the more demanding tasks?

Elementary School
- *Less demanding:* Create a diorama for Mother's Day about something you and your mom like to do.
- *More demanding:* Interview your mother about an event in her life that was important to her and write it up for her to keep on Mother's Day.

Middle School
- *Less demanding:* Draw a book cover for To Kill a Mockingbird.
- *More demanding:* Write an essay in which you discuss the relationship between Scout and her father. How does this relationship help tell the story?

High School
- *Less demanding:* Draw a picture of an electron.
- *More demanding:* Why is it difficult, unless you are a trained ninja, to break through a table with your hand? Explain and provide illustrations or graphs, using what you've learned in the unit on electrons.

The next chapter provides a step-by-step process and asks you to make instructional decisions about what to teach and why. Each step is designed to help you with those important decisions. Here are three reminders to keep in mind as you construct your assignment:

- An assignment is a kind of task distinguished by a prompt specifying a student product and a rubric.
- An assignment is *taught*. If it isn't, it's not an assignment. An instructional plan documents the teaching that transforms an assignment into learning.
- An assignment that is aligned to standards and involves students in meaningful work is worthwhile. An assignment that is not aligned to standards or relevant to the curriculum is a waste of time.

◆ ◆ ◆ ◆ ◆

Part 2

In the Classroom

This section describes how to craft an assignment, "instructional touchstones" that can be incorporated into many assignments, and how to sequence assignments into units and courses.

3

Crafting an Assignment

For a teacher trying to design an assignment, the ideal thing is
to put your students in a situation where they are challenged.

—Nate Kornell, quoted in Sparks, 2011, p. 6

Think of crafting an assignment as a design process, one that involves problem solving and innovation, form and function. You start to design your assignment with a vision, then acknowledge parameters in terms of resources, time, and energy. For example, you imagine an assignment that would help students learn how to read primary sources and exposes them to memoirs, letters, and accounts available in local and online history resources. You would consider what resources you have access to, what standards fit this assignment, where you are in the school year, and whether you are emphasizing new content and skills or ones already learned.

This chapter is a workbook to help you work through the process of crafting an assignment. The process of crafting an assignment involves you in "intentional teaching" because it forces you to be clear about your purposes and outcomes: what to teach, what you want students to learn, and how. (I have adapted elements of Dr. Ruth Mitchell's [1996] Standards in Practice protocol, in which teachers analyze tasks for alignment to standards, specifically Step 6.) You should consider crafting an assignment with other teachers. It's a good way to draw on each other's expertise and, as one teacher put it, "bounce off each other's ideas."

As a mental warm-up, consider the following as you begin to think about an assignment:

- *Address content using texts,* whether it's a single text to analyze or several texts used in research assignments.
- *Focus on the topics, issues, concepts, and facts embedded in an academic discipline.* For example, "romanticism," "manifest destiny," and "natural selection" are knowledge concepts in literature studies, social studies, and science, respectively.
- *Involve students in the practices they will apply while producing work.* For example, when studying a work of literature, students need to acquire skills in deconstructing specific types of texts. In social studies, they need skills in thinking like a historian and doing historical research, and, in science, skills in collecting and recording data.
- *Include behaviors expected in academic settings,* such as talking and listening with civility when participating in discussions, even when students disagree with someone. These skills aren't described in most state standards but are necessary for students to "learn how to learn."
- *Aim to prepare students for next-level courses.* For example, senior students need assignments that ask them to work more independently because in just a few months they will be in their first-year classes in college. Late-elementary students need to be able to manage a variety of texts and have experience in expository composition to manage the six-period day in middle school.
- *Emphasize cognitive skills,* such as the ability to draw conclusions, deduce a probable cause, and evaluate. These are examples of the cognitive skills applied throughout the academic continuum and in the workplace.
- *Think of products that are hands-on and relate to real-world situations.* For example, you might have students write technical and business documents, such as memos, proposals, and budget analyses. An oral assignment can become a campaign speech. Reading aloud can become a readers theater presentation. Students are motivated by

physical and hands-on products, such as a garden or a golf swing. (Products are covered in more detail later in this chapter.)

- *Involve essential learnings,* those "power" standards that are key to the academic curriculum because they are assessed on large-scale exams, such as state assessments or college exams, or because they are essential for next-level curriculum.
- *Address weighted standards in your assignments frequently.* Your state's assessment manual describes which standards are assessed and to what degree, so be sure to embed these in your assignments often. For example, one state weights vocabulary items at 28 percent in Grades 3 through 5. High school staff should also look for specific content and skills assessed on the SAT and the ACT and on college-placement and workplace exams.

College Ready, Career Ready: The Common Core State Standards

When referencing standards in the seven-step process of crafting an assignment, I refer here to the College and Career Ready Anchor Standards in the Common Core State Standards for English Language Arts. In this chapter and those that follow, the Anchor Standards are referred to by letter and number (for example, RL1). The letters represent the following categories:

- W = Writing
- L   = Language
- RL = Reading Literature
- RI = Reading Informational Text
- SL = Speaking and Listening

Consider these important features of the CCSS ELA, in both the Anchors and their grade-level versions, when crafting assignments, as they are key to aligning your work to the CCSS at any grade:

- Assignments should involve students in complex ideas embedded in texts.

- Students should develop skills in analyzing ideas and texts. *Analyze* is the dominant verb used in the CCSS grade-level standards after 5th grade. True, a verb is not a standard; yet verbs are starting points for creating the contexts for the cognitive and practical demands that make up an assignment. This essential thinking skill, whether it is in another form, such as "comparing" or "determining," involves the *ability to break down and examine* an idea or process.
- Assignments should include text-dependent questions or prompts to develop skills in extracting evidence from texts. (RL & RI1, 2, 3)
- The bulk of writing assignments should be multiparagraph compositions, such as reports and essays, rather than personal essays, memoirs, or narratives. (W1, 2, 7, 9)
- Speaking and listening are important components of literacy, and students should engage in a variety of speaking and listening venues, for example, seminars, debates, exhibitions, and monologues. (SL4, 6)
- Language involves more than just learning grammar and spelling rules. Assignments should help students become adept with language for different audiences and purposes, in speaking and writing. One of the most important skills students can learn is how to adjust language to fit their audience and purpose in speaking and writing. (L3)
- Assignments should be constructed to nudge students toward becoming independent learners. Helping students track their ability to manage assignments with increasing degrees of independence should be part of your instructional plan. (R10, W10, SL6)

Reflection Activity: Looking at Figure 3.1, what does the frequency of certain terms in the CCSS for Reading Informational Text mean to you as you think about crafting assignments?

Figure 3.1

Terms Used in Standards 1–9 for Reading Informational Text

Grade Level					Standard Number				
	1	2	3	4	5	6	7	8	9
6	cite analysis	determine summary	analyze	determine	analyze	determine	integrate	trace evaluate	compare contrast
7	cite analysis	determine analyze summary	analyze	determine analyze	analyze	determine	compare contrast	trace evaluate	analyze
8	cite analysis	determine analyze summary	analyze	determine analyze	analyze	determine	evaluate	delineate evaluate	analyze
9–10	cite analysis	determine summary	analyze	determine analyze	analyze	determine	analyze	delineate evaluate	analyze
11–12	cite analysis	determine analyze summary	analyze explain	determine analyze	analyze evaluate	determine	integrate evaluate	delineate evaluate	analyze

The Seven Steps

The process I recommend for crafting an assignment involves seven steps. This chapter provides guidance for six of the steps (the seventh step is detailed in Chapter 4, Instruction). The chart in Figure 3.2 summarizes the seven-step process. You might want to copy the chart and keep it in front of you as you move through the design process. You'll also find a blank version in Appendix A that you can use as you move from step to step, filling in the specific information related to the assignments you create.

Step 1: Identify Content and Skills

Jeanne Chall (2000) studied classroom instruction for decades to arrive at the conclusion that students learn when thinking and problem solving are taught alongside content. This is good advice to keep in mind as you use the start-up template in Figure 3.2 to help you begin thinking about the standards and content you want to involve in your assignment.

In Step 1, note that the template says "focus standards." These are the few standards involving content and skills you emphasize and teach explicitly and deeply. A single assignment taught with care and intensity cannot closely align with more than a few standards, perhaps no more than four or five. At the same time, one standard is probably not enough for an assignment. Teaching is not "coverage" or a process of "checking off" standards. The "ing" in teaching is a process of engagement and acquisition that results in learning. Focus standards designate the content and skills you expect students to demonstrate at "meets expectation" levels in their products. When you write your rubric, later in the process, you can lift language from the standards and from your prompt to create rubric descriptors. Doing so makes for close alignment between what you ask students to know and be able to do and how you evaluate their work or demonstration.

In this first step you start thinking about what skills you want students to learn or practice. Skills are usually described by verbs, such as *define, compare, solve,* and *design.* Skills can also be those technical activities that students engage in when producing a product, as designated by verbs such as *format* or *compute.* Auxiliary skills are those not usually found in content standards, such as planning a project or displaying civility during a discussion. These are important, too, so include them in your assignment when appropriate.

Figure 3.2 **Assignment Planning Guide**	
Steps	**Ask yourself . . .**
1. Identify content, focus standards, and skills.	What do you want students to learn? What academic content and skills do you want students to focus on? What standards? What other learning goals?
2. Determine a product.	What do you want students to turn in or perform as evidence of learning?
3. Identify demands and qualities.	What demands do you want to embed in the assignment? What qualities do you want to see in student work and performances?
4. Write a prompt.	This is the statement that asks students to do something.
5. Write a rubric.	What demands and qualities do you expect to see in a product for a passing grade?
6. Do your assignment.	Check your assignment. Revise if needed.
7. Make an instructional plan.	What resources and strategies will you use to guide students through the assignment? How will you teach demands and qualities? Make a calendar.

Use a pencil as you write down your start-up notes because you may change your mind as you think through the process. That's a good thing! To make this exercise worthwhile, think of an assignment you might teach in a few weeks. Here's an example:

Notes	
Content	civilization
Skills	define and explain
Other Skills	manage a multistep project; sort and select relevant details
Focus Standards	CCSS Anchors RI1, 4, and W2 (6–12 grades)

Continue to fill in the Assignment Planning Guide (copied from Appendix A) and proceed to the next step.

Step 2: Determine a Product

A product is something a student turns in or does to demonstrate learning specific to an assignment. Products document both learning and teaching: they provide tangible evidence of learning the skills and content specified in an assignment and of the effectiveness of instruction. Having dual evidence is important for a number of reasons. For one, products reveal students' strengths and weaknesses so that teachers can adapt instruction more strategically. As well, student products reveal the effectiveness of teaching choices. A class set of products can quickly reveal where instruction "took" and where it did not, and what was or was not taught. (Chapter 8 provides additional information about how products can be read as data and feedback.)

Not all products are appropriate for assignments. Worksheets, spelling tests, crossword puzzles, outlines, and notes, for example, are best used for activities that lead up to an assignment's product or tasks, in which your purpose is to give students practice or help them memorize, say, multiplication tables or grammar rules. Word games, for example, can build vocabulary skills and are good for teaching discrete skills. However, assignments are robust tasks and involve a larger context requiring students to apply multiple skills; so you need to assign products that allow for more complex demonstrations of learning.

In school and in college, the essay and the report are the most frequently assigned products. Accordingly, the CCSS have a language standard to address this area because academic protocol requires students to apply formal uses of language and structure in order to support a claim or a thesis. In most cases, students write or speak in three expository modes—argumentative, informational, and explanatory—and these are specified in the CCSS. Products that relate to the world outside of the classroom—what some call authentic products—are just variations on the academic products; examples include proposals, memos, and marketing presentations. For example, a proposal for a grant is an argumentative essay in a business suit and applies the same thinking and skills as those delineated in CCSS W1 for argumentation. Likewise, a memo that reports on monthly inventory employs the same thinking and structure as an informational product delineated in CCSS W2.

Of course, not all products need to involve writing something down. Oral and constructed products, such as demonstrations and scale models, can make assignments interesting and challenge students' thinking and skills.

Varying your products makes assignments more interesting over time, and it helps students if they have a variety of experiences from which to learn. Here's a list of products besides essays and reports that you might consider for your assignment:

- Animations
- Annotated bibliographies
- Community presentations
- Cost/benefit analyses
- Docent lecture
- Documentaries
- Games
- Inventions

- Maps
- Memos
- Patents
- Proposals
- Scale models and blueprints
- Skits
- Speeches

Reflection Activity: What products would you add to the list? Make a list of the products you have asked students to turn in. What kinds of products do your students produce? How varied are they? Does your list include hands-on or problem-based products?

Your notes should look like this as you proceed to Step 3:

Notes	
Content	civilization
Skills	define and explain
Other Skills	manage a multistep project; sort and select relevant details
Focus Standards	CCSS Anchors RI1, 4 and W2 (6–12 grades)
Product	essay

Continue to fill in the Assignment Planning Guide and proceed to the next step.

Step 3: Identify Demands and Qualities

Step 3 is a warm-up to crafting prompts and rubrics in the next steps. Now is the time to decide how demanding to make your assignment and what qualities you expect in student products. It is also a step in which you think about "thinking"—how to embed those intellectual challenges that motivate students to engage in skills. When composing this step, your knowledge and experience as well as your understanding of your students' academic progress become critical. Think of "demands" as the charge to do something with texts, content, and skills. Think of "qualities" as the features that describe how well students should demonstrate their ability to execute those demands. The confluence of demands and qualities embedded in an assignment establishes its rigor and at best ensures that an assignment isn't too easy, too hard, redundant, or off-standard.

Challenging assignments always involve reasoning or thinking about something—a topic, an idea, an issue, or a problem. Terry Roberts (1999) has written extensively on what it means to teach thinking, particularly through the seminar method. He identifies basic thinking processes as causation, transformations, classification, and qualifications, and complex thinking processes as problem solving, decision making, critical thinking, and creative thinking. To ensure that you are involving challenging cognitive skills in your assignments, check to see if you are embedding these thinking modes in your assignments.

Using the Assignment Planning Guide, Step 3, note a short list of demands and qualities. You will use the demands when you write a prompt in Step 4 and the qualities when you write a rubric in Step 5. Also note two or three standards that align to your demands and qualities. In this meta-process, you are ensuring your assignment is focused, aligned, and manageable. This short list sets the stage for a "going deep" instructional approach. A long list becomes overwhelming and irrelevant, even distracting, because it's not possible to teach with any depth a long list of demands and qualities in one assignment.

Choosing language to express demands and qualities is not always easy, so here are some guidelines:

Demands

- Use verbs as the focus of demands: e.g., *compare, define, construct*.
- Wrap content around the verb: e.g., Compare the conquests of Alexander the Great to Julius Caesar's.
- Align your demands to the Common Core State Standards or your state standards by adopting key words and phrases in your prompts.
- Moderate demands by choosing texts by their complexity, a feature distinguished by theme, idea, or syntax. (The CCSS emphasize "text complexity" as a feature that distinguishes rigorous instruction. See Appendix D for examples of texts.)
- Demands that involve reasoning are more demanding than those that do not. Ask "why," for example, rather than "what."
- Demands can be expressed as academic and workplace protocols. These protocols include specific language and skills involved in academic disciplines and workplace situations. For example, scientists are expected to say "hypothesis," not "claim," and to present their investigations in specific formats; workers are expected to write memos, not letters, to their bosses.
- Include behaviors that require students to master good habits necessary for academic and workplace participation. For example, you may want papers double-spaced, PowerPoint presentations in two colors, or speeches limited to three minutes. As well, students need to acquire the behaviors that allow them to discuss topics—for example, setting a goal to ask at least one on-task question during a seminar.

Qualities

- Qualities clarify what is valued in a product. Qualities are most often expressed as descriptors, such as *precise, accurately, consistently*, and *apt*. Use language that captures or describes what the best student work demonstrates: qualities involving both linguistic and cognitive fluency; demonstrating nuanced understandings, insightfulness, and reflection; and showing a deep regard for a topic or issue.

- Use visual models and examples to communicate qualities because a visual can sometimes communicate better than words. Showing students a professionally written book review, for example, can help them understand "how well."
- Include qualities of behaviors when appropriate. For example, a rubric for a seminar might include the quality of "responding respectfully."

Reflection Activity: What *qualities* would you expect to see in student work at the end of a school year in the following paired grades?
- 4th and 10th grades: a book review
- 8th and 11th grades: a speech
- 6th and 12th grades: a community service proposal
- 7th and 11th grades: a lab report

Your notes should look something like this:

Notes	
Content	civilization
Skills	define and explain
Other Skills	manage a multistep project; sort and select relevant details
Focus Standards	CCSS Anchors RI1, 4 and W2 (6–12 grades)
Product	essay
Demands	define, explain, organize ideas deductively, support ideas with citations
Qualities	credible, accurate, readable, well-developed logic

Continue to fill in the Assignment Planning Guide and proceed to the next step.

Step 4: Write a Prompt

It's time to write a prompt. A prompt is a statement that stimulates a response. It asks students to consider content in some way and produce a product related to that consideration. At this point, you have all the ingredients for writing a prompt statement, so what you do here is more about putting your thoughts together rather than starting from scratch. Here are some guidelines:

- Use a question to set up your prompt—for example, "Who is a hero?" "How does a computer store information?" "Are there good and bad calories?" "Why is Iago a sympathetic character—or why not?" A better question does not yield a simple yes or no answer.
- Use a quote to set up a response to your prompt.
- Lift language directly from the focus standards you've chosen, or turn the standard into a prompt.
- Challenge students with prompts that ask them to analyze complex texts for authors' purposes, structures, and methods. The CCSS emphasize textual analysis, so students need to acquire analytical skills to meet CCSS expectations.
- Describe a problem and ask students to solve it in some way. For example, ask students to write an editorial in which they examine a community problem related to trash and then present a solution. In science class, describe an issue about local water sources and ask them to write a report. Ask students to solve a design problem and produce a prototype—for example, a blueprint for a playground.
- Ask students to produce a workplace document, such as a brochure, report, memo, manual, needs assessment, survey, proposal, or customer communiqué.
- Ask students to synthesize research. These assignments include annotated bibliographies and reports in which they summarize research, points of view, or theories. Summarizing and synthesizing information are important academic practices, so be sure to embed these skills in your assignments so that students get lots of practice.

- Ask students to compare or evaluate ideas—academic, aesthetic, scientific, or practical—acting as an opinion writer or critic. This might be a feature article, for example, on the best irrigation techniques in a rural farm community or a critique of a film or restaurant.
- Ask students to improve on a product, service, or process and produce a blueprint or prototype.
- Hold mock events, such as a mock U.N. or Congress, and require students to speak on an issue.
- Put on an event, from proposal to production. This might include theater, film shows, or celebrations.
- Use prompts from state writing assessments and programs, such as AP or standardized tests, including the SAT and the ACT. These are usually available on websites as examples or released items.

An example from Re: Learning New Mexico illustrates how an assignment can trigger meaningful learning for students. On the Navajo reservation, young teens studied how their culture blends the practical needs of survival with ancient rituals. In response to an assignment prompt, one student documented practices surrounding the use of animals for food, shelter, clothing, and tools while respecting the life and spirit of the animal. His culminating product was a documentary video of an elder preparing a sheep, using every part of the animal for food or clothing.

Sources for Prompts

You don't have to write prompts from scratch. Several resources are available, including, as noted earlier, state department of education websites, where you can find prompts in released items or retest assessments. Newspapers, magazines, and other texts also offer prompt material, so keep a collection of prompts to use when you need them. Following are some examples of prompts from various sources (you will find more sample prompts in Appendix D).

Sample performance tasks in the Common Core State Standards rewritten as prompts (see CCSS ELA, 2001, Appendix B):

- Write an essay in which you compare and contrast coming-of-age stories by Christopher Paul Curtis (*Bud, Not Buddy*) and Louise Erdrich (*The Birchbark House*). (RL5.9, p. 70)
- Give a multimedia presentation in which you generate your own fractal geometric structure by following the multistep procedure for creating a Koch's curve. (RST6–8.3, p. 100)
- Write an essay in which you analyze Thomas Jefferson's *Declaration of Independence*, identifying its purpose and evaluating rhetorical features such as the listing of grievances. (RI11–12.9, p.171)

Prompts from state assessments:

- Steve and Michael were playing a number game. They turned the 15 cards shown below facedown. If Michael chooses one card, what is the probability that he will choose a card with an even number on it?
2 2 2 3 3 3 3 3 3 4 4 4 4 8 8
(Arkansas released item, 2003, Grade 4)
- How did the growth of U.S. manufacturing affect the country's international relations during the late nineteenth century? (California American History Assessment, released item, Grade 11)
- Often in works of literature, a character influences others in good or bad ways. From a work of literature you have read in or out of school, select a character who has the power to influence other characters in good or bad ways. In a well-developed composition, identify the character, describe how the character influences others in good or bad ways, and explain how the character's behavior is important to the work of literature. (Massachusetts retest item, 2007)
- Water-quality regulations are used to ensure the safety of public water. Two examples of these regulations are listed below:

– The use of lead pipes is prohibited.

– Standards describe what chemical levels in the water are safe and allowed.

a. Explain in detail two reasons why the government has established these types of regulations.

b. Identify two different sources you could use to get help or information if you thought your water supply was unsafe.

c. Explain the specific type(s) of information you could obtain from each source you identified in part b. (Kentucky released item, 1998–99, 8th grade Practical Living)

Prompts from newspapers and magazines:

• "What is an anti-hero?" (*USA Today*, 2/21/08)
• "Does money buy happiness?" (*New York Times*, 3/10/08)
• "What is art?" (*Washington Post* KidsPost, 9/22/2011)

The Literacy Design Collaborative

The Literacy Design Collaborative (LDC) has developed an instructional framework designed to help teachers in English, social studies, and science align their work to the CCSS ELA. The LDC framework consists of a collection of template prompts and instructional plans, called modules, aligned to CCSS. Teachers in English, social studies, and science codesign assignments by filling in blanks that specify content and a product. The framework is not canned assignments and instructional plans, but a ready-made prototype to provide guidance in crafting assignments. Using the templates helps ensure assignments are aligned to the Common Core State Standards. Another feature allows you to scaffold by adding demands to increase the complexity of the assignment. The use of templates allows for prompts to be used in any subject or grade and to cross borders that traditionally separate disciplines, grade levels, and geographic borders. Here is an example of a template aligned to CCSS Anchor Standards for reading and writing, and a teacher's filled-in version:

Task 12 (Informational or Explanatory/Definition L1, L2): [Insert question] After reading _____ (literature or informational texts), write a/an _____ (essay, report, or substitute) that defines _____ and explains _____ (content). Support your discussion with evidence from the text(s). **L2** What implications can you draw_____?

Prompt: After reading <u>articles and political documents on government lobbyists,</u> write a <u>report</u> that defines <u>"lobbying"</u> and explains <u>the role lobbyists play in our political system.</u> Support your discussion with evidence from your research. **L2** What implications can you draw <u>about the role of lobbying as a dynamic of the political process?</u>

> **Reflection Activity:** Using the LDC template prompt in the example, write your own assignment prompt. You can find more choices in the LDC Template Collection in Appendix D.

The Seminar Prompt

The National Paideia Center has developed an instructional system based on the Socratic seminar in which students ponder interesting questions that lead to equally interesting assignment prompts. For example, an elementary seminar lesson asks students to examine the metric system and ponder the following questions: "What is measurement?" "Where and why is the metric system used?" and "How are customary and metric units converted?" Students explore these questions through a process of experimentation and discussion; then they produce a written composition to answer the questions. Rubrics for speaking and listening and for composition help students understand what they must demonstrate during their discussions and in their compositions. They know what to do and how well to do it. (Chapter 4 includes more information about the Paideia seminar.)

Writing Your Prompt

It's time for you to coalesce the thinking and notes in Steps 1 to 3 and write a prompt. Write more than one version so that you can explore different possibilities and instructional opportunities. Look through the resources presented earlier for model prompts you can adapt to your needs, or write your own, drawing on your previous ideas recorded in the Assignment Planning Guide. Based on what you've learned so far, which of these two examples would you choose?

Sample Prompt 1: Would you agree that Mesopotamia was the first civilization? Write an essay in which you define "civilization" and explain your position based on your research.

Sample Prompt 2: Give a multimedia presentation in which you explain why Mesopotamia is called the "first civilization" by many historians.

Reflection Activity: After you've written various versions of your own prompt, check by asking yourself the following questions. Then choose one prompt for your Assignment Planning Guide template.

- How do your versions differ? Which one comes closest to what you want students to learn about and to do?
- Which one fits your curriculum scope and sequence best?
- Is this prompt worth teaching and spending time and energy on?
- Can this prompt be managed within a time frame that is doable and sustainable?

After reading the next section, come back to your prompt drafts and revise if necessary.

Problem Prompts

No matter how hard we try, sometimes a prompt just doesn't work. This happens for a variety of reasons, but if it doesn't work for us, it certainly won't work for students and should be revised or tossed. The bottom line is, prompts that are unclear, undoable, or unreadable are problem prompts.

Students can't meet your expectations or the expectations set in standards if they don't understand your assignments, starting with the prompt. Teachers who have worked with us have often surmised after their first couple of assignments that the prompt wasn't as clear or well stated as it should have been, and their students' work showed it. As well, if students do not understand *why* they are doing the assignment, they will not take the assignment seriously.

Often problem prompts suffer from a lack of specificity. Other times, they pack too much into one assignment. Sometimes we write well-stated prompts, but they aren't aligned to standards. The best prompts are a little like a good poem—every word counts. A good-to-great prompt creates an opportunity to learn a set of skills and content; it determines purpose. And there's a happy balance to be sought in crafting a prompt that makes the process of managing an assignment doable since any assignment involves multiple skills and cognitive manipulations. Here are examples of common problem prompts, followed by brief explanations of why the prompt is problematic and a revised version:

1. In a paragraph, describe the economic, political, and cultural features of the Native American society. Grade 6

This is an example of a "loaded prompt." Prompts like this one force students to write unwieldy paragraphs or skim content in an effort to be concise. As well, most assignments involving writing tasks aligned to the CCSS should be multiparagraph compositions, with the exception of summaries or free-write and reflection works. Another glaring problem is the lack of specificity. If content is too broad and involves several topics, students will write down anything they see that appears to relate to the topic: the so-called Native American society actually consisted of many societies. A better prompt would specify a single tribe.

Revision: Write a report in which you compare the two selected articles on the political structure of the Pueblo Indian community in northern New Mexico.

2. Research the Greek play Pyramus and Thisbe, *and then write a report that defines "star-crossed lovers." Support your discussion with evidence from your research. If you had friends who were in love and whose families disapproved, what advice would you give them? Grade 10*

Using the language and protocols of a discipline is important. In this prompt some things are off base. For one, it's not usual practice to "research" fictional works. One reads or analyzes a play or a novel but doesn't "research" such works. (You might research the history of a play but not a play as text.) Another problem is the product. An essay is a better product for this kind of analysis. Finally, the question could be addressed or discussed without reading the play and does not engage students in academic content or thinking.

Revision: It's your first day on the job at a local newspaper, and the editor has asked you to write a review in which you discuss the plights of star-crossed lovers in the local production of Romeo and Juliet *and the musical* West Side Story. *The editor expects to see several relevant examples from the two works to enliven the review and a treatment that will grab the readership's attention.*

3. Draw a picture of a house and talk to a classroom partner about your house.

This assignment was given in a secondary ESL class. Is this prompt worthy of an assignment? Some prompts should be relegated to the activity file or dumped altogether because they lack purpose and rigor. The following revision places the prompt in an arts appreciation class to be cotaught with an ESL teacher. It also shifts the prompt to a focus on discipline-based language skills more appropriate to high-school-age students.

Revision: Select a photograph or drawing of a house or building that incorporates the principles and techniques we studied. Give the class a four-minute presentation identifying and explaining these features in your selection.

4. Write an essay about the causes of the Civil War.

Recently I watched as a friend's kindergarten student cut out illustrated bears from a workbook page so she could put them on a pictorial bus and count them, in response to the question, "What if two bears go on the bus and one got off?" What struck me as odd was that I am sure I had the same workbook several decades ago! Similarly, the "causes of the Civil War" prompt never seems to go out of style. It's a cliché prompt, a type that appears over and over again, grade after grade, year after year. These are the ones that send high school students online to buy essays. Other such prompts include "my favorite animal" in elementary school and "Should students have to wear uniforms?" in middle school. Prompts dealing with token cultural features, personal experiences, and book reports, for example, rarely move or challenge students after the first encounter, if at all.

Revision: Drawing from what we have studied in the unit on the Civil War, write an editorial from the point of view of one of the political groups, arguing whether Maryland should enter the war.

5. Write about a trip you took this summer. Grades 4–5

Where's the product? This is an example of a "not yet successful" prompt. Again, this is a cliché prompt, but by assigning a product and designating an audience and a purpose, you can revise it. It doesn't hurt to add a reading or research dimension, too.

Revision: Create a three-minute media presentation in which you promote a travel site you have visited and researched for a community group. Include two to three visuals.

6. What is the most important challenge you have met? Read several personal challenge essays on the Internet. Then write an essay that explains a challenge you have had and how you met it. Support your discussion with evidence from your research. Grade 6

This is a prompt that wants to be academic but is really a personal essay based on other personal essays. It's challenging to score personal essays on traits such as "accuracy" because there's no way to evaluate accuracy of content or sources. You can only score them on style. As a general rule, assignments that don't require evidence from identifiable sources (reading, interviewing, notes, or tapes) belong in creative writing. The revision here attempts to place the notion of a real-world experience in a specific context while involving students in academic skills.

Revision: What are the challenges a person faces when making a career decision? Interview (take notes and record) someone who has made a career decision and write a feature article for the school newspaper explaining in detail what his or her most important challenge was and how your interviewee resolved it.

7. Draw portraits of four medieval types: peasant, merchant, priest, nobleman.

This example is a prompt that cautions us to be careful what we ask for. It was given in an 8th grade social studies class. Students did not take it seriously, turning in caricatures complete with cigars and medieval-looking Batmobiles. Silly work signals a weak prompt.

Revision: Choose a medieval persona you have researched and describe this persona in a monologue about a typical day in his or her life.

8. Should the United States have shot Osama bin Laden? Write an editorial in which you address this headline question.

This type of question, one linked closely to an emotional or current issue, can pose problems because in these cases students tend to write an uninformed opinion, not a researched or text-based response. If an issue is current, there probably isn't research to draw from, only speculation based on conversations or media reports rather than an informed position. Provide distance by using literature, particularly philosophy or fiction that addresses the values inherent in the issue but not the exact circumstances.

Revision: Is revenge ever allowable? Read Francis Bacon's essay "On Revenge," and then write a response to the question for an audience of peers. (This prompt is adapted from Volume 1 [1989] of the Touchstones Discussion Project. See www.touchstones.org.)

Clearly, it's worth the time and effort to craft a good prompt. The after effects of problem prompts are frustration, disengaged learners, and ineffective instruction. No one benefits from such prompts because they are, frankly, a waste of time and energy for both teachers and students. Getting the prompt right is critical because the prompt creates the context for instruction, the teaching and learning that you and your students will engage in over several days or weeks.

In Step 5 you will continue to clarify your expectations when you write a rubric for your prompt, further specifying demands and qualities. If your class turns in sloppy work or consistently misses some element of the assignment, you should first look at your prompt and then the rubric. Finally, a housekeeping reminder: Be sure to edit your prompts for grammatical and spelling errors. Then continue to fill in the Assignment Planning Guide and proceed to the next step.

Step 5: Write a Rubric

A prompt is not enough to communicate to students what your expectations are for their product. A prompt needs to partner with a rubric to convey with clarity your goals for them. The rubric is integral to the assignment; you don't yet have an assignment if you don't have both a prompt and a rubric.

A rubric has multiple functions, acting as a learning, teaching, and scoring guide. It's a learning guide for students because it answers their persistent question, "How do I get a passing grade?" It's a teaching guide because it describes what must be taught in "how well" terms; it's only fair to teach what is expected from students as stated in the rubric. And it's a scoring guide because you use the rubric to judge how closely a student met the expectations articulated in the rubric.

Making Rubrics Matter

A *rubric* is variously defined as "rules," "instructions," and "guidelines." In the classroom, a rubric is all these things: it establishes rules in that it makes transparent the traits expected in products, and it serves as instructions because it provides guidance on the "how well" features in a product.

Students and teachers can use a rubric as a reference throughout the production process—teachers teach the demands and qualities embedded in the rubric, and students follow the rubric almost like a recipe to produce their products. Rubrics provide a kind of advance organizer for students, giving them the guidance they need to perform to expectations. Without a prompt and a rubric that clearly set up the teaching and learning cycles, teachers and students can't do their work effectively.

Rubrics can come in many forms and formats and should be designed for a specific purpose. Holistic and analytic rubrics are commonly used in classroom and large-scale assessments, for example. A *holistic rubric* summarizes the demands and qualities expected in a product. An *analytic rubric* categorizes the features. You should choose the format that best suits your purpose and best conveys your expectations. There are many rubrics available on education websites to model or to adapt. For example, the Webb Scale is a rubric often used to determine the level of difficulty of items on assessments, but it can provide a useful reference for helping you determine appropriate descriptors of rigor when writing rubrics. (The Webb Scale can be found on a variety of online sites.)

University of Toronto researchers Lynn Sharratt and Michael Fullan (2012) conducted research showing that rubrics were most effective with students of all ages, from kindergarten through college, when teachers co-constructed them with students and when the rubric described only the "success criteria"; students were not interested in the criteria that described failure.

Rubrics in the classroom learning environment are not so much hard fact as a means of communicating expectations and providing feedback about learning progress. To best communicate your expectations, you have a number of design choices. A rubric can be a single statement of proficiency, describing what it takes to get a passing grade, or it can describe several levels of performances, as in state assessment rubrics and rubrics for major assignments. A single statement is holistic in that it summarizes the key features in a few sentences rather than in a grid containing multiple categories and statements. The important point here, again, is that you design a rubric to further clarify a prompt, emphasizing what the expectations are for a specific assignment as it sits in the curriculum continuum. For example, a rubric written in the first week of school should describe fewer demands and different qualities than one written in the middle or last term. Together, the prompt and the rubric articulate expectations in clear, unambiguous terms as much as possible. For this reason, it usually doesn't work to use a rubric you haven't written or edited. Use a generic rubric only after aligning it with your assignment and making sure it includes the content, skills, and qualities you choose to focus on. Beware of so-called rubrics that only list "to do" criteria, not qualities.

As stated earlier, a rubric acts as an instructional guide because it also describes the learning goals you have to teach. That is, if you want students to draw to "accurate scale," then you must teach them how to do that and be accurate. In Step 7 (covered in Chapter 4), you will use your rubric to make an instructional plan, linking the demands and qualities you've specified in the rubric to your choice of teaching strategies and practices. This congruence among prompt, rubric, and instruction makes for strong alignment. Here's an example of a high school history teacher's holistic rubric that is written in prose yet conveys multiple expectations without those grids that isolate criteria into boxes:

> *A* **range:** This paper is outstanding in form and content. The thesis is clear and insightful; it expands in a new way on ideas presented in the course. The evidence presented in support of the argument is carefully chosen and deftly handled. The argument is not only unified and coherent but also complex and nuanced.

> *B* **range:** This paper's thesis is clear; the argument is coherent and presents evidence in support of its points. The argument shows comprehension of the material and manifests critical thinking about the issues raised in the course. The paper is reasonably well written and proofread. The argument, while coherent, does not have the complexity, the insight, or the integrated structure of an *A* paper.

C **range:** This paper has some but not all of the components of an argumentative essay (e.g., thesis, evidence, coherent structure); for example, it may offer a thesis of some kind, but it presents no evidence to support this thesis; or it may present an incoherent thesis; or it may simply repeat points made in class without an overall argument. Such a paper is poorly organized, written, and proofread. A paper will fall below a *C* if it lacks more than one of the basic components of an argumentative essay.

Reflection Activity: Compare the following two rubrics for the way they express "meets expectations." Ask yourself: To what degree does each address content and skills, demands and qualities? Is the rubric a "to do" list or a rubric that clarifies "how well," or maybe something in between? Does the rubric align with the CCSS for Speaking and Listening?

Rubric #1: Debate Rubric

Rate each criterion: 1–10

- Appearance of team.

- Opening statements were well organized.

- Team member addressed remarks to the audience.

- Opening statement was not read from cards.

- Both team members participated equally in opening statement.

- Students spoke loud enough to be heard.

- Rebuttal was specific to arguments made in the opposing team's opening statement.

- Both team members participated equally in the rebuttal.

- Answers to audience questions were well thought out.

- Respect was shown throughout the debate for the opposing team (no name calling, interruptions, etc.).

(*Source:* http://712educators.about.com/cs/rubrics/l/blrubricdebate.htm)

Rubric #2 Seminar: Speaking and Listening (Meets Expectations)

Attention: Looks at the person speaking during most of the discussion.

Engagement: Rarely talks while another is speaking.

Articulation: Occasionally takes notes related to the ideas being discussed; gives way to another as a way of sharing the talk time.

Explanation: Makes clear and accurate statements; generally speaks at appropriate pace, volume; uses relevant vocabulary and grammar.

Expansion: Provides points/statements about the discussion topic, noting details related to sequence, category, purpose, or point of view.

Connection: Refers to the text or another relevant source; considers another point of view and states personal bias; asks authentic questions; paraphrases what else has been said.

(*Source:* Robers & Billings, 2012, p. 60)

Whether it's a sentence or a few bullets or multileveled or a grid, a rubric should clearly and concisely state the *qualities* you expect to see in student work. Of course, these qualities relate to the charge you gave students in the assignment prompt and the standards that informed that charge.

Writing a rubric has its challenges, asking you to bring to bear your experience with a grade level, your understanding of curriculum standards, your teaching motives and purposes, and your language skills. Collaborating with colleagues can make rubric-writing easier and provides great professional development as it takes advantage of shared experiences and builds consensus about what expectations should be for students. For even more transparency and consensus, write rubrics with your students, using the connections among content, standards, and expectations as a lesson in goal-setting.

Classroom-based rubrics serve a different purpose than rubrics for summative assessments, which are about measurement at scale. Assignment rubrics live in the classroom and are generated from a context for learning and should reflect the intentional instructional choices you make when you craft an assignment and teach it. Factors such as the standards or skills and content you chose to emphasize in your assignment and the time of year you taught it can and should be weighted in an assignment rubric. A rubric written for an assignment in the first week of school should not look like a rubric for an assignment at the end of the year because expectations later on should involve higher levels of quality and competence from students.

Common rubrics for some skill sets, particularly grammar and conventions, can help students internalize expectations from class to class, course to course. In this case, they learn that using language effectively and well is not just a requirement in English class but is expected in all classes and courses, as well as outside of school. Also, common rubrics save you from having to repeat these traits in your assignment rubrics. Common rubrics should be constructed by staff to communicate a consensus about specific skills. For example, a common, grade-appropriate rubric in elementary school for language conventions would scaffold the skills, such as capitalization and punctuation, from grade to grade and be applied in every subject. (The PARCC Framework provides a useful analysis of the changes in demands from grade to grade. See www.parcconline.org.) It's far clearer to students if a staff agrees on what "good use of grammar and conventions" is—and in more specific terms.

When rubrics set and communicate clear goals, teachers and students speak the same language about performance. When rubrics help make assignments transparent in this way, they make the cycle of learning and grading fair. For example, an assignment given at the beginning of the year might focus on one or two elements in the rubric, whereas later in the year a similar assignment would specify multiple elements. Rather than "dumbing down" a rubric, it's better to limit the demands and qualities until students learn to manage them. You can always add elements to your rubrics as the year progresses and as your students' competencies develop. If you apply this rubric scaffolding technique, you can better control the pace and rhythm of the learning progression.

Accordingly, you should view scores derived from assignment rubrics as feedback more than hard data. What you should not do, though, in the scoring process is adjust the rubric for an individual student. If you write rubrics to fit your instructional needs, your expectations and student outcomes will converge. As you craft the assignment prompt and the rubric, continue to ask yourself a set of guiding questions: What do I need students to learn now? How will this help them in the future? How much can they manage? What do I need to reteach? The following discussion covers some ways to craft rubrics for different purposes.

Form and Function: A Rubric for Every Purpose

In crafting a rubric, your first step is to decide what format best communicates to students the attributes of achievement on a specific assignment. Your first consideration is how to categorize achievement. The usual 4-3-2-1 format is always a choice, but there are others. For example, Mitchell cites a rubric for a state assessment that uses the headings "beginning," "developing," "accomplished," and "exemplary" (1996, p. 47). The latter format conveys a different impression than the numerical one, perhaps indicating that learning is a process rather than a series of final events. Some rubrics draw from the apprenticeship model with terms that convey a natural progression in acquiring skills—for example, those taken from the guilds: "novice," "apprentice," and "master." If you want a rubric that conveys the possibility of second chances, you might consider terms such as "exemplary," "commendable," and "needs revision."

However, not all rubrics need categories. As in the high school history sample, you can convey in a single statement what it means to "pass." The following example for students writing a proposal increases demands from grade to grade using a single statement. The key qualities are "convincing" and "logical."

Elementary: Your proposal must be *convincing and logical,* providing three reasons supported by your survey.

Middle School: Your proposal must be *convincing* and pro-vide a *detailed rationale*, supported by original data from your survey.

High School: Your proposal must be *convincing* and *address all elements* of a proposal, including a needs assessment, a project time line, and a budget.

The assignment prompt developed earlier in this chapter in which students are to define and explain the concept of "civilization" still needs a rubric to become an assignment. Here, a one-level rubric partners with the prompt to make the assignment whole:

Prompt: What features determine a "civilization"? Write an essay in which you define "civilization" and explain its fea-tures, drawing from our unit on ancient societies. Would you claim that any of these societies were not civilizations?

Rubric: Your essay should demonstrate the following quali-ties to receive a passing score: (1) a researched definition of "civilization"; (2) a detailed explanation with references to unit texts; (3) a convincing argument focused on the question; (4) organization using three-point logic; and (4) a readable, neat copy, including a 3 on the ELA mechanics rubric. This is a two-week assignment.

The *analytical rubric* is another possible format. Unlike the one-level rubric, the analytical rubric describes two or more levels and describes demands and qualities in categories, as does the six-trait rubric and many rubrics for summative assessments. Figure 3.3 shows an analytical rubric for a 5th grade social studies assignment. In this assignment, all attributes must be met to receive a score of "commendable" or "exemplary." Note that the "novice" level is written as suggestions for revision rather than failure.

For most students, words alone, no matter how well chosen, aren't sufficient to convey "how well," and so *visual rubrics* are useful. Product examples or models help students understand, in visual terms, the demands and qualities you are expecting. Examples can be student work from other classes or models of professional works from magazines, books, and other sources. Point out and explain the demands and qualities in your rubric as you analyze examples to help students see what words can't quite explain. This is most true of qualities. Reading a convincing argument and seeing insightful artworks are the only ways students can develop an understanding of those attributes. It's good instruction, too. Examples and models of specific details in your rubric, such as "effective transitions," help students understand criteria as they produce their products.

Figure 3.3			
Sample Analytical Rubric for Social Studies			
Westward ho! Read primary documents (in library) about the pioneer experience. Prepare and recite a monologue in which you take on the persona of a pioneer figure.			
Exemplary	Accurately presents the persona's viewpoint in factual terms and captures the emotional/social contexts as well.	Monologue is not more than three minutes. Skillfully uses stylistic devices to capture the language and tone appropriate to the persona.	Writer's Habits: Takes relevant research notes; uses primary and secondary textual evidence with a high degree of relevance.
Commendable	Accurately presents the persona's viewpoint in factual terms with some emotional/social references or effects.	Monologue is not more than three minutes. Uses language and tone appropriate to the persona.	Writer's Habits: Takes research notes; uses primary and secondary textual evidence to support claim.
Novice	Claims and sources should be checked for accuracy. Does not represent the viewpoint appropriately.	Monologue should be revised to be no more than three minutes. Use of language and tone are not appropriate to the persona.	Where are the writer's notes? Were notes taken from primary and secondary sources? Points need to be supported with textual evidence.

Workplace rubrics take on a different form and format but nevertheless accomplish many of the same purposes as a school rubric. They include job descriptions, performance reviews, and task analyses. Projects or units, such as teaching a class or managing a theater production or community event, would be good assignments for using the format of a professional performance review instead of a school rubric. Teachers can enliven assignment prompts and rubrics by making connections to the world of work. You can do this by writing assignments as memorandums or posting job descriptions.

Reflection Activity: Analyze job or career descriptions in the career section of the newspaper for work-world "expectations." Think about how you might create job descriptions or performance reviews for projects. A good source is the skill maps for English and social studies at the Partnership for 21st Century Skills (www.21stcenturyskills.org).

Writing Your Rubric

As you write your rubric, refer to your Assignment Planning Guide, Step 3, where you noted what qualities you want students to display in their products. These traits set the stage for your rubric. If you wish to revise them, do that now. If you are finding it a challenge to come up with language, look at the Common Core State Standards and your state standards or other resources. For example, language to describe good and excellent student work in science can be found in your state standards, and for a more global reference you could refer to the National Science Standards; in addition, Advanced Placement rubrics are a good source for several subjects.

In writing your rubric, follow these guidelines:

- Decide what format—holistic or analytical—best serves your purposes for this assignment.
- Focus on what's important for students to demonstrate on this assignment.
- Be sure your rubric emphasizes qualities.

Continue to fill in the Assignment Planning Guide and proceed to the next step.

Step 6: Do the Assignment

Doing your own assignment is a necessary step and good practice. By testing your own assignment, you can anticipate where your students may struggle or misunderstand and plan accordingly. As you work through your assignment, note what instructional strategies might apply and make sure you have the resources you need to teach the assignment. Then, consider whether you have all the instructional skills to teach your assignment. If not, draw on the expertise of your colleagues or ask for assistance and professional development.

You may find that you have asked for more or less than you initially thought or that the assignment is just too confusing. In any case, if the assignment doesn't make sense or fails to ask for the level of demand and qualities you intended, you need to revise it. One brave teacher had another teacher grade her paper using her rubric, without telling her it was her paper, not a student's. The good news is she scored "advanced." She said the experience made her highly conscious of her students' needs and how they might experience the assignment, allowing her to prepare better than she would have otherwise.

In her book *Creating High-Quality Classroom Assignments*, Lindsay Clare Matsumura cautions teachers not to look for "unmitigated success in every way at first try" and "to expect a certain amount of trial and error" (2005, p. 2). Similarly, I urge you to try out different types of assignments and approaches and not to be held captive by the need for perfection. Each assignment is an opportunity for both you and your students to improve; and even in an assignment that doesn't fulfill all its promise, students will learn more than doing worksheets or low-demand activities. Matsumura's book provides useful rubrics to help you think about features relevant to assignments, including texts and prompts. Her rubrics are also useful as self-monitoring tools to ensure assignments are worth teaching.

◆ ◆ ◆ ◆ ◆

You are now ready to continue with Step 7 and develop an instructional plan. Chapter 4 will help you do so.

4

Instruction

A more useful practice is to organize strategies to provide a framework of effective instructional design.

—Marzano, 2003, p. 81

Instruction—the ways in which teachers employ strategies, practices, and tools to teach—is ultimately about learning. Synonyms for *teaching* include *coaching*, and for *learning* the idea of *absorbing* or *acquiring* knowledge and skill. The "ing" in teaching assignments, then, is the act of coaching students through the experience of absorbing knowledge and acquiring skills as they complete an assignment's product.

Your next step is to design a plan by making deliberate instructional choices that support the assignment you wrote in Chapter 3, in which you crafted an assignment's prompt and rubric. Your plan creates a series of instructional events as conditions for learning and leads students to complete the product embedded in the assignment. An assignment taught with intention *and* attention is dynamic, and it animates students to interact with ideas and people in a variety of ways in their pursuit of knowledge.

The first part of this chapter discusses the importance of equity and excellence as foundations on which to make choices. You will also find a description of instructional touchstones, or practices and tools that work with any assignment. These instructional touchstones, when used strategically, can help you imbue your instruction with learning experiences that improve students' abilities to manage academic tasks and challenge them at the same time. Finally, you will complete Step 7 in your Assignment Planning Guide and record those important instructional choices. (You may want to have your copy of the CCSS ELA on hand as you work through this chapter. See page 7 in the CCSS [2001] to read an explanation of key features.)

A well-crafted assignment does not ensure outcomes, but it certainly sets the stage for results. Ultimately students depend on your instruction to learn and produce the quality product you've assigned them. When you teach intentionally and with skill, your students will grow intellectually and in other ways, becoming more independent as learners and, not inconsequentially, meeting expectations embedded in standards and the curriculum.

Instruction: The Great Equalizer

During a convening in which teachers shared their experiences teaching assignments developed through the Literacy Design Collaborative, more than one teacher commented that "even our struggling students" were motivated to address the challenging questions and tasks included in their assignments. A science teacher who had never taught literacy practices—much less an essay—in her classes taught an assignment containing the question, "Are cell phones dangerous?" She chose this question because it was "relevant" to teens and gave her instructional opportunities to teach how to investigate an issue scientifically. To address the question, students explored electromagnetism using both literacy and scientific skills in ways this science teacher had not brought into her instruction when she taught the topic before. She taught scientific thinking through the processes of research, experimentation, and writing an argumentative composition. The teacher reported that it was "payday" when, shortly after completing their assignments, students saw the same topic addressed in national newspapers and media reports. She said that her students became even more motivated to read, write, and debate other science topics.

When you challenge all students to think and provide them with opportunities to build their knowledge base, grow intellectually, and develop necessary skills, you transform a belief in the equality of opportunity into "equality of instruction," a phrase attributed to Frances Wright (1829), a 19th-century social reformer who believed in the power of education to make a difference in the lives of individuals and society. Teaching all students to think strategically and critically is to teach equitably. In doing so, you help students gradually acquire competence to move on to the next assignment, the next course, and the next opportunity. This foundational belief in the power of effective instruction to transform motivates both teachers and students to take on intellectual and academic challenges and to set high expectations for achievement. It's that important.

Kathy, a history teacher, related how she came to understand that even "apathetic" seniors who had skated through their high school years can "rise to the occasion" if an assignment challenges them and is purposeful. In her assignment, students researched voting rights—who votes, who doesn't, and what the impact of voting had on their community and themselves. She related how students became "animated" and put up with the more tiresome editing and revision work she demanded in order to complete the research assignment on time and with good results. Her strategy was practical—do what it takes to ensure each student is successful *on the same assignment.* She chose an assignment that was as challenging to her honors students as it was to the less skilled students. She did not differentiate the challenge, just the instruction. Even if some were more successful than others, all students gained a good understanding of the issue and acquired skills in the process. What differed, for the most part, was not so much her strategies—all students were taught note-taking methods, for example—but her pacing. Although she similarly taught each step of the research and writing process, she gave more direction and time to those who needed more direct instruction, sometimes explicitly and at other times through demonstration. For example, she gave templates to students who struggled with the composing process, and she coached students who didn't have the means to arrange face-to-face interviews with community officials on how to make a call to ask for an interview.

Kathy is an example of a teacher who acts on her belief in "equality of instruction." She sets expectations for all students, AP and non-AP, to learn the content and acquire the skills to participate in the study of history. She does that by keeping demands constant but providing instructional intervention and guidance as students need it. As a result, Kathy's instructional choices enable students of different needs to meet the challenges she embeds in her assignments. Her determination to teach her students, all 205 of them, can show us that "equality of instruction" is more than an ideal. It is a theory of action manifested through technique, characterized by the following attributes:

- Equality of instruction pushes (and prods) students forward in a learning trajectory, and well-crafted assignments set the stage for instruction that teaches with purpose.
- Equality of instruction does not depend on a student's talent or background to manage and do well on assignments. Instead, an assignment provides an opportunity to learn and strives to ensure all students are challenged to new levels of achievement.
- Likewise, when students struggle with practical skills (for example, composition, grammar, computation, execution, or diction), instruction targets their needs explicitly while respecting their abilities to think about complex ideas and problems and to participate in the curriculum.

If you believe in equality of instruction, you will be tenacious in finding instructional practices and supports to ensure students engage in rigorous assignments that prepare them to participate in and contribute to a society that values ideas, literacy, and critical thinking. Following are four instructional touchstones you can rely on to infuse instruction with intellectual and practical challenges.

Instructional Touchstones

Mr. C., a 5th grade teacher, designed an assignment as a culminating task for a term unit on the U.S. civil rights movement of the 1950s–60s. For the first few days, students engaged in a variety of activities to reexamine the topic, rereading some of the materials they had explored in the unit, including media accounts from the period and old *Life* magazine articles Mr. C. had found at the local flea market. He taught them note-taking methods they could use while listening during a lecture or an interview and when reading and viewing materials. His assignment prompt asked students to prepare and give an oral and technologically based presentation comparing accounts of two Freedom Riders' experiences drawn from at least three different primary sources. He focused his instruction on Common Core State Standards RI4, RI7, and SL4. Steps in his instructional plan took their cue from the demands and qualities set in the assignment's prompt and rubric:

- Giving students exercises that asked them to paraphrase the prompt and rubric.
- Teaching research and reading skills by revisiting sources and news-account tapes with the prompt in mind.
- Using visual as well as print material to explore a topic.
- Teaching skills appropriate to the prompt and rubric (for example, note-taking as a function of research and organizing points into a structure of thought).
- Engaging students in small-group discussions based on questions he composed to help students deeply explore perspectives and issues.
- Teaching students how to discern a credible source.
- Conducting a seminar to help students work through their thinking about the topic.
- Using templates and other explicit tools for those who needed them.
- Arranging a "penny reading" during which students read passages from their research at a parent night gathering. (At penny readings, which occurred in 19th-century American rural towns, people read a passage for a penny to community members, many of whom were illiterate, at town meetings.)
- Creating a schedule that allowed students' parents or community members to attend presentations.

Mr. C.'s lesson plan includes four touchstone practices: foreshadowing, seminar, lecture, and purposeful technology. If you include one or more of these instructional touchstones in your plan, you will create variety and opportunities for students to learn as they move through an assignment cycle.

This list starts with foreshadowing, or those practices that anticipate next learning steps and, in this case, prepare students to take on an assignment. It is a critical first step in any instructional plan that accompanies an assignment.

Foreshadowing an Assignment

A high school student facing the prospect of writing an essay for his history class was asked to react to the assignment, the first step in the LDC instructional ladder. After a class review of the assignment and an initial "yeegads," he wrote, "This task is asking me to do some research in several different ways to explain Imperialism . . . I SAY BRING IT ON." When the time comes to introduce an assignment, students need to know what's ahead and, as one student put it, what the "game plan" is. Ausubel's classic "advance organizer" tells us that learners need to know the game plan in order to manage any learning process in school or in life outside of school (Ausubel, 1963). An advance organizer can also serve as a bridge between old material and new material, and it is a strategy that positions students to build on previously learned content and skills while acquiring new ones. Too often this first step is skipped or done lightly. However, if you approach it thoroughly, your students will be more likely to stay on task and arrive with a product that is focused.

Here are practices teachers have used to help students prepare to engage in an assignment. You can do any of them with your class or have students work on them individually:

- Paraphrase the prompt and rubric.
- Show the connections between learned content and skills and the new ones.

- Make a plan with a time line in which students identify stages and due dates.
- Deconstruct and analyze professional examples of products similar to the assignment's product.
- Submit daily "exit" passes that act as evidence of learning the main skill taught that day.

Reflection Activity: During a unit on Alexander the Great, how might you prepare students for an assignment involving research and making a map detailing his path through Asia?

Seminar: Meaningful Discourse

Talking about something—how an electric bulb lights up, or World War II, or the current environmental crisis, or Hamlet's obsessions—is probably the oldest way to learn. Talk comes in a variety of forms—discussion, conversation, and conferencing, for example—in and out of the classroom. To truly learn from any form of talk, students need to acquire skills in speaking, listening, and language usage as well as behaviors that allow for an exchange of ideas.

Seminars are well-planned events that focus on ideas and values embedded in texts and teach the conduct of discourse along the way. Teachers are always in control but are not the "knowers." During seminars students learn from each other by exploring ideas and hearing how others grapple with them (Roberts, 1999; Zeiderman, 1984). Seminars that expose students to a wide range of experiences and to peers whose level of success in schooling varies widely can create a group dynamic that would not happen otherwise, as students gain respect for each other's thoughts and contributions to the discussion.

I cannot say enough about the importance of discussion, especially seminars, as a key event in assignment teaching because meaningful discussion promotes thinking, and thinking is the ultimate product of any assignment. A genuine discussion requires skills that must be developed and encouraged "in order that, at some stage, students and all of us can speak with one another about those issues and concerns which engage us most profoundly" (Zeiderman, 1984, p. 79). In a genuine discussion, particularly in a seminar, thinking is a natural event. Billings and Roberts (2012), who developed the Paideia method for a seminar, define thinking as the "ability to explain and manipulate a text, a set of interrelated ideas, often represented in a human artifact." They go on to say that the "key to teaching thinking, then, is to teach it as one of a cluster of interrelated skills: as part of reading and writing as well as speaking and listening" (p. 1). This view of thinking fits perfectly in a classroom where learning is based on texts and textual evidence. (See CCSS RL1 and RI1.)

During a seminar, students contemplate a text while they sit in a circle together. The teacher sits among them but does not participate except to reread a text aloud or to start discussion with a question. She probably asks a text-dependent question to start with, such as, "What word is most important in this first paragraph, and why?" Students learn to moderate the group without raising hands to speak or to work for short periods in pair-shares. As the seminar proceeds, the teacher remains silent, only asking two or three questions to guide students to the text and into their discussion. The last seminar question is always "essential" in that there is no yes or no answer.

In classrooms where students come with a wide range of literacy skills, seminar is one of the most powerful ways to support all learners in one setting because they are of equal status; there is no tracking or differentiation in the seminar circle. Students learn to work together, to hear, literally, how their peers arrive at a conclusion, for instance, or analyze a text. Novice or struggling students can learn from their more language-adept peers and observe how they articulate their thinking as they interact. On the other hand, skilled students may be practicing "obedient purposelessness" and benefit from listening to students who are not tuned in to the familiar or clichéd views of the "A" student. (Dr. William G. Perry, Director of the Harvard Reading-Study Center, uses the phrase "obedient purposelessness" to describe study and reading practices that follow the rules too closely and, as a result, waste time. See www.people.fas.harvard.edu/~lipoff/miscellaneous/exams

.html.) Discussions involving students with a range of school and real-world experiences allow each participant to learn from others and to develop a tolerance for different viewpoints. In the process, all, including the teacher, absorb and acquire understandings of an issue or topic embedded in an assignment.

The Lecture: College-Ready Instruction

In contrast to seminar is the lecture, a much maligned instructional strategy but one that is prevalent in college and even the workplace. Someone—a professor or a supervisor or a hired gun—stands in front of a group and lectures the audience (students, workers) on a topic or procedure. As in the movie *The Paper Chase*, professors often build their reputations on their lecturing skills. Used appropriately, a *short* lecture can prepare students for college courses and provide them with necessary content for an assignment.

Every five years or so, I visit the high school I attended, and during the last visit I saw that a lecture hall had been built so that students could become comfortable in such a setting. I sat in on a lecture by a history teacher during which he periodically stopped and suggested that students "take this note" to help them know when something stated in a lecture was worth recording. A younger returning alumna told me that she found her 300-student freshman lecture courses at a large university much less daunting than many of her friends as a result of this training. The lecture, like most things in life, needs to be dealt out in moderation but offers opportunities for students to gain confidence in such settings and acquire good listening and literacy practices they will use all their lives.

> **Reflection Activity:** How might you incorporate seminars and lectures to engage students in a sensitive local or historical issue that they will write about in an editorial?

Technology

We live in an era of technology, even "hypertechnology," in which gadgets have inserted themselves into the daily functions of the learning and teaching environment. Teachers who contributed to *Teaching 2030* describe "a new learning ecology," one in which "we expect to see not only students having regular interactions with community members, subject area experts, and peers from other locales, but also to see teachers having similar interactions about content, curriculum, pedagogy, and assessment with distant teacher colleagues, researchers, and other experts" (Berry et al., 2011, p. 63). Today, some advanced form of technology is found in every classroom and school. Teaching assignments, especially those involving literacy practices, can surely benefit from technology. Clearly, word processing makes composing, through its drafting and editing phases, a much more doable activity for students than typing on a clumsy typewriter or, as I had to do, writing final drafts in script with an ink pen. Audio and video technologies allow students to acquire speaking and listening skills as they might when producing radio-talks and interviewing sources. For example, students in an American Paideia school participate in seminars about common texts with students in Sweden, using Skype as their medium. (For more information about the National Paideia Center's seminar method, go to www.paideia.org.)

I do not argue the merits of technology as a teaching tool, but I do want to emphasize that the critical point is how it is used and the choices you make to support your instruction. That is, use technology when it enhances the quality of student work and not just for its own sake.

Used purposefully, technology undoubtedly serves teachers in their efforts to help students access knowledge and acquire skills. As well, students need to acquire skills in using different technologies to become informed and to communicate, produce, and innovate. CCSS Reading Anchor 7 is clear on this point, stating that students should "integrate and evaluate content presented in diverse media and formats, including visually and quantitatively, as well as in words." However, technology cannot make up for a weak assignment. If students use computers to engage in weak assignments, then the only learning that's accomplished is practice on keyboarding or video games.

When, as reported in a recent national news account, a district invests heavily in technology but fails to get gains on student assessments, the problem probably lies in the tasks students are asked to engage in rather than the technology (Richtel, 2011). Technology can be put to good use in the classroom as it is in the workplace: to speed up and enhance processes, such as editing or researching. The great advantage of technology is that it can enable students to participate in complex assignments even when they struggle with specific skills. CAST, a Harvard research center that supports the Universal Design for Learning, a "set of principles for curriculum design that give all individuals opportunity to learn" (see www.cast.org/udl/), also promotes the use of technology to support all students in the learning process. The center's director, David Rose (n.d.), argues that students' struggle to understand texts is not so much a student problem as it is a problem with the way educators present texts. That is, if teachers present texts in an accessible form or format, students can read and acquire understanding. Likewise, technology can help students communicate their understandings in speech or writing. Technology is clearly a present and future solution to providing instructional supports that adapt to student needs. Those classrooms that are equipped with interactive whiteboards and laptops and where students use pads and cell phone apps for learning are advantaged, no doubt.

However, not all classrooms have these advantages, so it is prudent to consider what staff can do to enhance instruction with the most basic technologies and equipment. Ideally the time will come when every student has a laptop or other portable computer, at least while in school; but until then you don't need advanced technologies to engage students in challenging assignments. Not so long ago, before many of these advanced technologies existed, teachers relied on very few gadgets. For many of us who taught before the cell phone era, technology was limited to an overhead and a tape recorder. If we were lucky, we had access to a camera or video equipment. Nevertheless, these old-fashioned technologies provided opportunities to help students manage challenging tasks.

The following examples present two images of how two pieces of equipment can help you engage students in practices that build their competence and independence as learners as you teach an assignment.

The first involves a classroom in Los Angeles where I observed middle school students conducting their own revision conferences using an overhead projector. It was an expectation in this school that students take responsibility for their own learning as often as appropriate. During my visit, a student who needed help with an opening paragraph put his paper on the overhead projector while a group of peers helped him refine his work. They clearly were comfortable with this routine and engaged in purposeful, self-directed learning. Simple but effective! Using just an old overhead projector, students worked together, applying multiple literacy practices—reading, writing, speaking, and listening—to solve a problem and, in the process, improve their ability to communicate in an academic setting.

I was struck by these students' collaboration, which seemed to me to resemble that of employees in the tech sector. Tech workplaces, often called "campuses," seem more like Summerhill—the "original alternative school," which challenged the construct of traditional schooling methods (see www. summerhillschool.co.uk/)—than an imposing office. These workplace settings feature movable furniture, gathering places, and atriums where employees come together to strategize, plan, and problem solve; they're filled with the latest electronic gadgets. Nevertheless, during visits to a few of these campuses I have noticed that technology wasn't necessarily visible where the work took shape when there was thinking to do—to solve problems, analyze products, or review data. Instead of sitting in front of computers, employees talked with each other, uninhibited by gadgets, to analyze problems and strategize. Sometimes they worked in rooms with a table and an interactive whiteboard or just stood around in a circle, free-associating. Eventually, they used technology to continue the work, but their initial efforts were done without technology.

What if students learned in environments where they could move easily between human-generated interactions and technology? The good news is that there are such schools, where students are learning with the help of technology and are learning to use technology to communicate their ideas to peers and those outside of the school. Quest to Learn, a middle school in New York City, is a good example of how technology used purposefully engages and teaches (see http://q2l.org/). At the elementary level, In2Books is a Web-based service that connects students with epals to exchange letters about books (see www.in2books.epals.com).

The second example of effective use of existing equipment demonstrates that dedicated teachers find ways to ensure that students engage in assignments and often use something as simple as a tape recorder to make that happen. It involves a special education teacher who was determined to include her highly challenged students in a middle school's Anchor assignment involving a written book review. She adapted by having her students interview each other using a tape recorder about a favorite story. Then she transcribed what they said onto paper. When these students heard themselves on tape, they laughed at their own voice, but they also expressed how excited they were to have participated with their less challenged peers on the Anchor assignment. Annie, one of the students, stopped someone she knew in the hallway at break and told her friend why she liked her book.

> **Reflection Activity:** What technologies do you have in your classroom or school to enhance or assist with an assignment involving research or data collection, reading the *Odyssey*, or building a scale model?

Step 7: Write an Instructional Plan

Now that you have progressed through six steps of crafting an assignment (as detailed in Chapter 3) and have a prompt and a rubric ready to be taught, your final step is to create an instructional plan. In the process, you will make choices to employ the instructional touchstones and other strategies that support the "ing" in the teaching of your assignment.

Your plan is a sequence of short, targeted instructional events, each of which is defined by a purpose and supported by an activity. Altogether, the plan leads students to completion of their product.

In most ways, you already determined your instructional plan when you wrote your assignment prompt and rubric. You must teach what you ask for. That is, because the assignment prompt and rubric state the demands and qualities students must demonstrate to meet expectations, you must teach how to incorporate those demands and qualities in their work. Your job now is to "extract" from your assignment's prompt and rubric the places where the instructional steps should occur so that students can produce the product. Imagine your assignment is a play. What is the first act? What is the second? How many acts do students need to complete this "play"—that is, to turn in their finished product?

Your plan should take into account factors that might influence the degree to which you demonstrate or emphasize some set of skills or content. For example, you probably would have fewer explicit steps at the end of the year on an assignment type that you have taught throughout the year than on one new to your students.

This sample 9th grade assignment occurs during a unit on archetype heroes in which students read early works of literature involving mythology:

Assignment: Write an essay in which you analyze how Homer used physical environments to portray and develop characteristics embodied in *Ulysses*. What effect does this use of setting have on the work?

Rubric: Apply your understanding of archetypes in literature to explain and elaborate on the prompt. Your two- to three-page essay should demonstrate the following qualities to receive a passing score: (1) a detailed analysis that addresses the prompt and question; (2) a credible thesis; (3) a well-organized, logical structure; (4) relevant and supportive textual evidence; and (5) a readable copy with few errors. This is a two-week assignment.

Figure 4.1 shows the partially completed plan for this assignment. Prompted by the first part of the plan, fill out the second half. You should, of course, design your own chart or method for documenting your instructional plan, adding details that help you manage and pace the assignment. For example, you may want to include a column noting specific standards that apply to each instructional event. The challenge is to keep your plan manageable while helping you think through and document your work. As important as planning is, the goal is to have you spend time teaching your students rather than working on a plan.

Figure 4.1		
Sample Instructional Plan		
The first steps are filled in. What instructional events and activities would you continue with to ensure students complete the assignment?		
Step	**Instructional Event**	**Activity**
1	Review prompt and rubric	Deconstruct an essay sample in whole and small groups
2	Explore "hero" and "physical environment"	10-minute segment from *Odyssey* animation Seminar on prompt question
3	Review composing process	Lecture on constructing a thesis statement and opening paragraph
4	Organize composition	Provide templates
5	Conference on templates (logic, structure)	Conference on thesis and organizer
Step	**Instructional Event**	**Activity**
6		
7		
8		
9		
10	Essays due—no lesson	The Essayists—Students read passages from their essays during Scholars Night

LDC's Instructional Ladder

The Literacy Design Collaborative has developed a prototype plan called an "instructional ladder" housed in the LDC module template. The instructional ladder is a series of instructional events that lead students to completion of a written product in response to a prompt involving one or more texts. Each event is termed a "minitask" and addresses a literacy practice, such as note-taking or editing. The minitasks also provide teachers with multiple opportunities to acquire scores as well as give feedback to students on their progress. Each minitask is accompanied by a two-point rubric, ensuring that students receive timely feedback along the way to completion of their products. The minitasks also ensure that instruction consists of more than a series of activities because the tasks are collected, scored, and noted. Minitask products allow for formative feedback because a teacher can take a pulse and correct any misunderstandings based on student products. The purpose of the minitask system is to make sure students are, in fact, on task and on target and are being taught incremental skills in reading and writing.

The LDC instructional ladder clusters literacy skills into four sections and starts with a bridging conversation about the assignment to ensure that students know what they are to do and why. Throughout the ladder, minitasks create the instructional events that lead to completion of the product. One group involves reading and another involves writing because all LDC tasks are designed to produce writing in response to reading. Figure 4.2 shows two sample minitasks with a short scoring guide. One minitask focuses on vocabulary development to ensure students acquire the vocabulary to manage not only the reading of texts but language involving content and the discipline. In the second minitask, students draft their first attempt to put it all together—the reading and the writing.

LDC gives you two options: you can use the prototype instructional ladder or construct you own version by editing the prototype ladder to fit your instructional needs and purposes. This feature gives teachers guidance and saves time. No one likes to go home to face the prospects of writing up an assignment and an instructional plan after dinner or before school.

Figure 4.2

Sample LDC Minitasks

These are examples of short, incremental assignments that lead to completion of a composition written in response to reading texts.

Minitask for Note-taking	Minitask Scoring Guide	Minitask for Creating a Draft	Minitask Scoring Guide
Prompt: In your notebook, identify key words or phrases as you read and define them denotatively and connotatively in context of the passage in the work you are reading. Add terms we identified as the "language of the discipline." *Product:* Vocabulary notebook entries	*Meets:* • Identifies vocabulary, phrases and notes their denotative meaning and, if applicable, their meaning in context of the passage(s). • Writes in readable prose. *Not yet:* Attempts to meet the criteria for "meets"	Write an initial draft complete with opening, development, and closing; insert and cite textual evidence. Identify competing argument(s).	Completes a readable draft with all elements on task.

Lesson Study

A lesson study is a great way to work collaboratively to craft and teach assignments. Consequently, a lesson study involves teachers in a number of decisions and collective thinking about what to teach and how best to address improvement. There are a number of resources and protocols for lesson studies, such as the ones described by the Lesson Study Research Group (www.tc.edu/lessonstudy/tools.html). The elements of a successful lesson study involve small teams of teachers who work together to learn something about the effectiveness or their instruction by

- Identifying an area of student achievement for improvement.
- Researching how to achieve improvement.
- Redesigning an assignment to accomplish improvement and a method for assessing whether such improvement occurred.
- Testing an assignment, activity, or assessment.
- Demonstrating a lesson or assignment to other teachers.
- Repeating the process two to three times per year.

Some Planning Don'ts . . . and Do's

As you plan and deliver instruction, pay attention to these don'ts and do's my colleagues and I have learned from experience and culled from research:

- *Don't talk too much while you instruct.* That is, plan your instruction to limit teacher talk and to allow students to do the work. This recommendation doesn't mean a lecture now and then isn't a good experience, particularly if it involves note-taking. However, too often teachers do the bulk of the talking and in the process give away answers or limit students' abilities to explore ideas and practice skills (Billings & Roberts, 2012).
- *Don't stray from your plan.* If you engage students in instructional strategies or programs that don't support the assignment, they get lost and lose momentum (Marzano, 2003).

- *Don't be too repetitive.* Vary your instructional events from assignment to assignment; this keeps the classroom experience more interesting and motivating (Danielson, 1996).
- *Do give students multiple opportunities to learn content and skills.* That may mean repeating a skill set in an assignment but with different content or approach; for example, skills employed in writing an academic essay could also be practiced when creating a documentary (Marzano, 2003).
- *Do let your students make mistakes.* The first way we learn is through trial and error. As well, design a grading system that allows for reteaching and relearning. When you build in trial-and-error instruction, you will be rewarded when students finally say, "I get it!" (Stiggins et al., 2006).
- *Do show your enthusiasm for learning, even when it's a struggle.* Your enjoyment of learning and your enthusiasm will transfer to your students.

❖ ❖ ❖ ❖ ❖

5

Sequencing Assignments to Design Units and Courses

To learn and to practice what is learned time and again is pleasure, is it not?

—Confucius

Designing courses following the guidelines presented in this book involves a process of organizing content into units in which you then situate assignments. This design process creates coherence and continuity and supports a learning progression when each unit contains one or more assignments that ratchet up demands. Assignments are the stuff of units and courses; they deliver on the big ideas, themes, concepts, topics, or issues that constitute a course. Like a Ukrainian nesting egg, a course is a nested structure: assignments sit inside a unit, and units sit inside a course. A well-sequenced course connects content and skills from assignment to assignment and unit to unit. As a result, when this sequence also presents learning experiences along a progression of complexity, coursework prepares students for the next grade level and keeps its sights on college and career. In this way, students engage in multiple opportunities to acquire, practice, and apply content and skills. You are undoubtedly familiar with some methods of designing units and courses, so the point of this chapter is to present some ways to sequence assignments within units and courses in order to create a learning progression and generate instructional power.

The goal of a sequence is to leverage each assignment to create a synergy that supports students in their efforts to become increasingly independent and confident learners. Clearly, well-crafted assignments are necessary ingredients for well-crafted units and courses. By making close connections from assignment to assignment and from unit to unit, a course becomes a greater power than its individual parts, just like the famous formula says. Such power propels students forward in their learning progression. An effective course, like effective teaching, is built on the belief that students can learn challenging content and skills, and it creates opportunities for success. As students become increasingly capable and confident, they take pride in their growing abilities.

Doug Reeves (2006) reminds us that "exquisitely formatted planning documents are worse than a waste of time. They are in fact inversely related to student achievement" (p. ix). The processes and formats described in this book may look like the simple charts they are, but they have evolved out of my own and colleagues' efforts to save time while focusing planning on the act of teaching.

Five Design Principles

As in any design endeavor, principles help guide decisions. Five principles guide this book's approach to unit and course design incorporating assignments:

1. *Thoughtful engagement.* Students engage in academic thinking, practices, and products appropriate to the discipline.

2. *Literacy as common practice.* Students engage frequently in reading, writing, listening, and speaking and language usage.

3. *Value.* Units and courses are worth doing because they are connected to standards and long-term goals, such as college readiness or next-level coursework.

4. *Manageability.* Units and courses are manageable in time and effort for both teachers and students.

5. *Pressure gently applied.* A course is designed as a continuum that moves students through increasingly rigorous work. (Vicki Phillips, director of education at the Gates Foundation, coined the phrase "pressure

gently applied" during her years as a superintendent to describe how educators and systems should persist in delivering high-quality curriculum.)

These principles articulate a belief in the power of strategically designed curriculum; each principle supports coherence and continuity in a unit and course by underscoring the premise that sequenced assignments and units are more powerful than randomly delivered ones. Keep these principles in mind while you plan units and coursework, as each principle informs your choices in creating meaningful work for students.

Reflection Activity: What other principles guide your thinking when you design a course? How might a syllabus reflect those principles?

Designing a Course Chart

Courses revolve around a controlling idea, topic, concept, period of time, or some other large body of knowledge in a discipline. Units break down the course using subcategories linked by some rationale and strive to build knowledge and skill over time—a semester or a year in most cases—thereby creating sustained connections. For example, a virtual public school has designed a freshman English course with six units involving literary "journeys." The first unit focuses on the "journey into the unknown," in which students read science fiction and write a major essay. Subsequent units continue with this notion of a journey into different genres.

Charts are excellent organizers for this work; they provide a helpful overview in which you determine the general components that make up a course and the sequence of content. When setting up a course chart, the first step involves deciding on the number and character of units (if you are designing a single unit, you only need two rows, one for your headings and the other for your components). It's usual to start planning with big ideas or standards, but you can also start with products, texts, essential questions, or any other heading you feel guides the progression of the course. Eventually, you will come back to this first draft to add details of each unit to include some combination of assignments, activities, and assessments, but you must first decide on the overarching content and learning goals that make up the course. As you move through this chapter, you will find a set of methods for thinking through the elements of a course and sequencing assignments to produce an effective learning experience.

The course chart in Figure 5.1 is an example of a draft for an interdisciplinary middle school science and literacy course developed by the National Paideia Center. The top row identifies the elements of the course, and the left column, the unit themes, or "big ideas." The course designates a unit each quarter anchored by essential questions that are the basis for seminars and assignments. In this course, the controlling idea involves scientific concepts for a general middle school course on the human body in which literature augments and enriches the scientific content. Students not only examine and explore basic scientific concepts—measurement, the human body, heredity, and evolution—but do so through both fiction and nonfiction texts.

Reflection Activity: How does your method of building a course compare to this one?

The following sections cover methods for starting the design process for a unit. In the first, you start with student products rather than standards or content, which come later in the design process. The second method starts with a focus text. Whatever method you use for designing a unit, repeat it for each succeeding unit to develop a course, as in Figure 5.1. These methods help you sequence demands by increasing

- Text complexity from assignment to assignment, unit to unit.
- Challenges in managing the production of products.
- Complexity of content and ideas using questions or themes.
- Demands using the guild construct of novice to expert.
- Demands by varying assignments from simple to complex, short to long.

Figure 5.1

Sample Course Overview Chart

Big Ideas	CCSS/State Standards	Related Ideas	Essential Qs (Seminar Qs)	Texts—Excerpts and Works	LDC Assignments	Assessments
Q1 Measurement Unit	Focus on Common Core Literacy Standards & State Science Standards	• Time • Distance • Change • Data • Scientific tools	Why measure? How do scientists think?	The Beaufort Wind Scale Article on the scientific method	Task 23—Essay (Comparison) Task 7—Report (Problem-Solution)	Self-assessment Peer assessment Teacher assessment
Q2 Human Body Unit		• Gender • Growth & development • Body systems • Interdependence	What makes us human? How do the systems in the body relate?	Excerpts: • Hippocrates • Galen • Harvey • Lewis Thomas	Task 13—Essay (Description) Task 9—Article (Cause & Effect)	Self-assessment Peer assessment Teacher assessment

(continued on next page)

Figure 5.1

Sample Course Overview Chart *(continued)*

Big Ideas	CCSS/State Standards	Related Ideas	Essential Qs (Seminar Qs)	Texts— Excerpts and Works	LDC Assignments	Assessments
Q3 Heredity and Genetics Unit Scientific Ethics Unit		• Family • Transference • Trait • Genetic engineering • Ethics	Who are you? When should scientists be allowed to experiment on humans?	"Heredity" (poem) *Frankenstein*	Task 12—Essay (Definition) Task 6—Essay (Argumentative/ Evaluation)	Self-assessment Peer assessment Teacher assessment
Q4 Evolution Unit		• Time • Deep time • Change • Species • Individual	What is a species? Can an individual evolve?	"How Flowers Changed the World" (Loren Eiseley)	Task 19— Annotated Bibliography (Synthesis) Task 9—Essay (Cause & Effect)	Self-assessment Peer assessment Teacher assessment

Starting with Products

When you start by deciding what types of products students will complete in a unit or course, you want to make sure that this list includes a variety of products. As well, you should include products that are explicitly described in the CCSS or your state standards, particularly those in writing and speaking. For example, CCSS W2 states that students should "write informational/ explanatory texts." I suggest that at least one product per term involve writing in response to reading and that this is probably the one for which you would craft an assignment. A type of product signals the form and function of future assignments. That is, an essay signals an assignment involving writing in response to reading. A speech signals an assignment involving rhetorical and speaking principles. A project involves an assignment in which students manage multiple tasks. When you start with products, you ensure there is sufficient variety and evidence of learning.

As an example, look at the following unit designed by a history teacher and his students. This is one of eight units for the course. They started with a course chart's last column, titled "Assignment Products," then worked their way through the other columns to complete the overview of the unit. In this first unit you see a pattern that remains throughout the course, in which students complete at least three types of products: a project, an annotated bibliography, and an essay. This pattern continues in each unit, although the content changes. Using a pattern is a clever design feature because it allows students to become familiar with and internalize sets of skills over a course while addressing different topics. By the end of the year, his students were able to manage each assignment type with little intervention even though the challenges were more difficult. This design feature builds into the course a learning progression that aims to build independence in learners (see Common Core State Standards for English Language Arts, 2001, p. 7). Once they decided on the products, they mapped backward and identified other elements of the unit: content, essential questions, and focus standards. Note that one of the unit assignments is a district Anchor assignment.

Unit Content: Historical perspectives and concept
1620–1787

Essential Question: How does progress affect society? How do we know our accomplishments were right?

Focus Standards: SS.CM.HS.06.01 Identify and understand the effects of 19th century reform movements on American life in the early 20th century.

Assignment Products:

1. Project (My America): Annotated bibliography

2. Anchor Assignment: Essay

Assessments: Oral and written quizzes, Unit pre- and post-tests

In this unit design the authors—teacher and students—paced the work over six weeks, allowing two weeks each for the project and essay, a week for the bibliography, and time for in-class assessments. Each product is a place-holder for an assignment that will be taught during the unit. By starting with products, the design process focuses the unit and course on outcomes and ensures that students will produce a variety of products.

Reflection Activity: What products would you designate for your first four weeks of school to ensure that students receive instruction in CCSS literacy skills, particularly writing in response to reading and analysis?

Starting with a Master Text

Another way to start designing a unit is by selecting a master text that will serve as the centerpiece for a short series of unit assignments. The quality of the text you choose is an important factor because it will determine the quality of ideas students will engage in and the depth of your instruction. A quality text, according to Matsumura, "is one that has enough thematic or plot complexity, or complexity in the language or imagery used by an author, to support meaningful classroom discussions and written responses" (2005,

p. 2). If you select a quality text, you also set the stage for instruction that will engage students in ideas and skills.

Content Landscaping

Content landscaping is a collaborative protocol that starts with a team identifying a text, which can be a book, a painting, or a graphic. The team free-associates to make connections that create the basis for prompts, much like Steps 1–3 in the Assignment Planning Guide in Chapter 3 (see Figure 3.2). Carlton Jordan, an independent consultant who provides coaching in literacy and curriculum design, coined the term and developed the protocol as a professional learning activity that draws on team members' knowledge base to determine meaningful content for a unit. (It works particularly well with an interdisciplinary team.) After identifying a text, team members analyze its relevance for the course, asking questions such as these: Is the theme meaningful? What is the primary conflict? What is the author's intent? (Matsumura, 2005, pp. 10–18). If the text passes this scrutiny, it becomes the focus text. The team then creates a "landscape" around the text through a process of free association based on a set of categories. For example, the poem "The Road Not Taken" by Robert Frost might call to mind an artwork, another work of literature, or a theme. The terms that emerge from free associating make up the content that surrounds the text, or a "content landscape." Content landscaping is fun to do, as well as being a productive professional development activity. Here's one way to conduct a content landscaping session and to get thinking loosened up and on paper:

- Create a table with two columns and at least five rows (you can always add rows later).
- In the left column identify categories. In the example in Figure 5.2, you see "Themes, concepts," "Events," "Artworks," and other categories.
- In Row 1, Column 2, write the title of a focus text: a book, poem, play, article, research text, or visual document.

Figure 5.2	
Sample Content Landscaping Chart	
Focus text	U.S. Constitution
Themes, concepts	(Liberty) freedom, inalienable rights, rule of law, representation, rights versus privileges, (interpretation,) (arguments)
Events	Revolutionary War, civil rights movement, emancipation, Equal Rights Amendment
Artworks	*Ode to the Common Man, Born to Be Free*
Other texts	*Ain't I a Woman,* (*Tinker v. Des Moines,*) *Brown v. Board of Education*
Products	Essay, (debate,) readers theater, (brief)
Activities	Field trip to history museum, invite a constitutional lawyer, Socratic seminar

- In Row 2, write down any themes, concepts, ideas, or values that come to mind.
- In Row 3, do the same to identify connections with current or historical events.
- In Row 4, identify artworks, including music, paintings, and photography.
- In Row 5, identify other texts related to the focus text.
- In Row 6, identify products.
- Other rows might include activities, skills, or standards.

Once the free-association chart is completed, circle one item in each row. Use these circled words to construct a prompt that includes one or more of these terms. Repeat to construct a second prompt. You now have two assignments for your unit. You also have a list of supporting materials for activities to enliven student interest in the focus text and to develop a deeper understanding.

In the example in Figure 5.2, the group identified a set of associative items from the list and then composed two assignment prompts for a unit on the United States Constitution:

Assignment 1: What were the major arguments for and against presented by the Supreme Court in *Tinker v. Des Moines?* Write a 500-word brief in which you summarize these arguments.

Assignment 2: Debate the meaning of "liberty" in the preamble of the Constitution in which you relate a past or current event to your interpretation.

Text Complexity

When choosing texts, consider how you might use sequencing to increase text complexity over time within a course. The CCSS place "emphasis on the sophistication of what students read and the skill with which they read" and goes on to explain that "whatever they are reading, students must also show a steadily growing ability to discern more from and make fuller use of text, including making an increasing number of connections among ideas and between texts, considering a wider range of textual evidence, and becoming more sensitive to inconsistencies, ambiguities, and poor reasoning in texts" (Common Core State Standards ELA, 2001, p. 8).

Appendix B of the CCSS provides grade-by-grade lists of sample texts to help you calibrate appropriate text complexity in your sequencing design. Another resource is one many teachers are familiar with, the Lexile scale, which rates texts by syntactic and other linguistic cues, as more or less difficult on a scale from 300 to 1100. This scale can be useful for identifying texts on a single topic with varying degrees of complexity. For example, you may want an easier-to-read text on a science subject that's difficult, or you may want a variety of leveled texts for a class in order to make it possible for all students to read about a topic or subject.

Using Multiple Assignments for a Single Product

Longer products, such as proposals or detailed reports, provide good experiences for students when they are ready to manage multiple elements involved in the production. If you want students to develop a longer product, you may need to break the production sequence into a few short assignments. For example, a research project might involve several assignments. One might be an interview; another, an annotated bibliography; and the last, a presentation to a local panel accompanied by a written report. What changes in each assignment is the skill set: the first assignment involves listening and note-taking; the second, reading and research; the third, speaking after planning a presentation; and the fourth, a written report. This multiassignment unit is a particularly good approach for year-end units because students have acquired the experience and skills to take on some of the work themselves while you focus instruction on refining those skills.

Documentaries, community reports, and school journals are examples of projects that make good multiassignment units. Projects are most relevant when they are authentic in that they involve students in the world outside of school and in activities such as experimentation, exploration, community service, internships, construction, and public presentations. Planning and writing multiple assignments requires a lot of work, but a well-executed project can help students develop skills and the patience they need to manage work in college and the workplace, so one or two projects a year is probably a good experience to include in your course. The challenge is to build a project around a sequence of assignments, not just activities.

There are also programmatic resources that involve authentic practices or "doing" at scale in which you can build in assignments. I list only a few here to get you thinking:

- Project-based learning, or PBL, which for decades has given teachers a comprehensive method for designing hands-on experiences, is still a relevant resource today. (See www.edvisions.org.)
- Debate, mock trials, and mock U.N. are experiences that can involve more than one assignment to help students prepare for their roles in these settings. Each has regional and competitive programs.
- Micro-society is a program that involves students in simulating a society, complete with its legal, financial, and cultural institutions. Isleta Elementary School in El Paso has developed a mini-society

in which assignments include having students "teach" members of the immigrant community how to participate in their new society, including such skills as how to write a check and how to apply for a driver's license. (See www.microsociety.org.)

- School and community gardens support learning by doing by having students grow foods and other plants. After growing them, students can transform their crops into edible products for sale at the local market. The Edible Schoolyard is a classic version of these programs (see www.edibleschoolyard.org).

- School-based studios are hands-on settings where students learn a wide range of skills, including academic, technological, and business skills. For example, in an animation studio at a Los Angeles high school, students learned how to work complex computerized programs to produce animated products. They also learned to apply literacy practices and learned what makes a good story. They had to market their products and sell them to local businesses and vendors.

Ratcheting Up in Sequence

To increase complexity from assignment to assignment or unit to unit is not an easy design or instructional feat. Increasing complexity is a key feature in the Common Core State Standards and the two frameworks for national assessments, PARCC (Partnership for Assessment of Readiness for College and Careers) and SBAC (SMARTER Balanced Assessment Consortium).

Increasing Complexity by Increasing Demands

To better understand how the CCSS spiral and increase demands, you should analyze the standards from grade to grade. (The PARCC Draft Framework, released August 2011 at www.parcconline.org, provides a useful analysis that highlights the changes in language from grade to grade.) For example, note how a standard in writing changes from 4th grade to 5th grade:

4b. Provide *reasons* that are supported by facts and details.

5b. Provide *logically ordered reasons* that are supported by facts and details.

To help teachers do this, the LDC framework provides levels—statements that add rigor to a prompt, to increase the challenge from assignment to assignment. To plot complexity using the LDC template tasks, you repeat a template but raise the demand to a higher level than the last one by adding a Level 2 or 3. Compare the following two LDC prompts; one was taught early in the year, the other, later. Students first acquired the basic skills of argumentation before they took on the added demand of addressing counterclaims.

> **Task 1 Social Studies Example:** After researching academic articles on censorship, write an editorial that argues your position, pro or con, on the use of filters by schools. Support your position with evidence from your research. (Argumentation/Analysis)

> **Task 2 Social Studies Example:** After researching academic articles on student rights, write an editorial that argues your position, pro or con, on the right to wear armbands in school. Support your position with evidence from your research. **L2:** Be sure to acknowledge competing views. (Argumentation/Analysis)

The first assignment creates opportunities to teach basic argumentation, asking students to form a claim and to give two or three reasons why they do or don't support student rights to wear armbands in school. In the second, they must elaborate more, by managing a comparison composition and addressing competing positions.

When you intentionally plan a sequence of assignments and units that raise demands, you apply pressure gently but firmly. In this way, students can grow intellectually and internalize skills without feeling overwhelmed.

Reflection Activity: Consider the texts students are reading this year in your class. Order them from less to more complex and note why you've identified them as such. Check to see that you are, in fact, progressively challenging students with different types and ranges of texts. If you don't see this progression, revise your list so that you do.

Short to Long, Simple to Complex

Another way to sequence assignments within a unit or from unit to unit involves varying them by type, length, and difficulty. I call this method SLSC, or "short to long, simple to complex." Using these features as a frame for determining the sequential order of assignments allows you to create a more varied and interesting sequence, so you do not have to pace assignments in a monotonous series of simple to complex. Instead, you can mix it up by following a longer assignment with a shorter one to give students a breather and time to focus on a smaller set of skills. Likewise, you might give a longer assignment but with simple demands or a short assignment with complex demands.

SLSC combinations pair two types of cognitive demands—simple and complex—with two types of structural demands—short and long:

- *Simple* demands include the more literal cognitive activities, cued by verbs such as *describe, sequence, paraphrase* and *copy*, and the basic thinking processes of causation, transformation, classification, and qualification.
- *Complex* cognitive demands are signaled by verbs such as *compare, analyze,* and *synthesize* and complex thinking processes, including problem solving, decision making, critical thinking, and creative thinking. These demands can be made manageable by keeping the product short if students have not yet mastered them. Simple cognitive demands can be complicated by inserting multiple steps or applications.

- *Short* assignments are short in both length and time frame. They are good for introducing a new skill or refreshing already learned ones and for moving students to complex demands without overwhelming them with length.
- *Long* assignments are long in both length and time frame. They allow students to apply simpler skills and content with more elaboration or technique or to put it all together, demonstrating that they can manage a set of skills and content. Projects and multiple-draft assignments fit into this category.

In a sequence, for example, whether it's a unit with more than one assignment or a course sequence, start with a short assignment with simple demands as an introductory experience and then follow with a short one with more complex demands. Continue with another short, simple assignment, followed by a complex, short assignment, and ending with a long, complex assignment that culminates the unit.

To ascertain what sequence is best for your unit, you analyze student work along the way. Such an analysis will tell you whether students need more direct instruction or more practice. Using this technique you can make learning possible for students and lead them to new heights in their academic competence. One educator calls this a "waxing and waning" strategy.

Example 1: At the beginning of the year you assign this task: *Write a three-paragraph composition relating* (simple) *an account of an event.* Later in the year, to raise the demand, you complicate the prompt by asking students to compare two events in multiple paragraphs: *Write a 200-word news article* (short) *in which you compare* (complex) *two candidates on an issue.* The prompt is still short, but you've added the more rigorous cognitive step of "comparing."

Example 2: *Create a PowerPoint presentation on water usage in your home.* This task is simple because it's straightforward. It involves collecting data and then presenting them, using technological and communication skills. Depending on the skill levels of the students, this could be technologically complex but cognitively simple. To raise the demand, you might rewrite the prompt to this: *Compare water usage in 10 homes in your community.*

As students acquire content and skills, you want to combine the "long" and "complex" quads, as in this example:

Example 3: *Write a detailed analysis* (long) *comparing two characters who confront moral or philosophical conflicts, and explain how they resolve them. What can you draw from these characters and their approaches to conflict?* (complex) *Choose characters from any of the three books we read this term.*

Reflection Activity: Think of tasks for your grade level of choice using these combinations:
- Short/simple (e.g., three paragraphs, description)
- Short/complex (e.g., three paragraphs, explanation)
- Long/simple (e.g., essay, synthesis)
- Long/complex (e.g., research paper, comparison)

Spiraling

A version of ratcheting up demands is "spiraling." In a unit, you track the learning progression from assignment to assignment while overlapping some content and skills in order to provide practice on those areas where students need refinement. In a course, you overlap and ratchet up from unit to unit. Spiraling gives students multiple opportunities to acquire and practice content and skills and to take on new challenges. Spiraling is not always a straight line upward on the complexity trajectory. At times you might want to vary elements within an assignment, rather than all elements, in order to make an assignment manageable or to emphasize some skill. However, over the time span of the course, students engage in a general progression of complexity and demands.

When you spiral a course, you once again focus on assignments. The design goal is to involve pairs of assignments, either in concurrent units or in some other sequence, that overlap in demands with different content. The first assignment introduces the basic skill set and content, while the second adds more challenge. In a course, assignments in a series of units should not be at the same level of demand; the last assignment in the unit should be more demanding in some way than the first. Here are three ways to use texts to accomplish this effect:

- Use a familiar text to provide practice on skill sets but call for a challenging product to teach new skills, such as an analytical essay or a multipart science exhibit.
- Use a difficult text but keep the product less difficult to allow you to teach students skills necessary to read denser or unfamiliar types of texts, such as a long novel or a technical document.
- Use a variety of texts at different complexity levels so that students of all reading abilities can access themes or information while learning strategies to manage the more difficult ones. To manage multiple texts on a single theme, you may need your librarian to help you, or you can seek online resources.

Creating Complexity of Thought with an Open Question

Using open-ended questions that stimulate thinking is another good way to manage spiraling in a course. As in the Paideia course in Figure 5.1, questions set the stage for assignments and activities within each unit. A good question provokes examination of texts and ideas, and sometimes situations and conditions. Literal questions do not go very far because you can answer them with a yes or no. Literal questions are useful for classroom discussion and quizzes, but open-ended and essential questions give a unit or assignment intellectual heft. Billings and Roberts (2012) define an essential question as "a question that can't be answered." These are questions that demand reasoned speculation and exploration because there is no solid evidence for a factual answer. Here are examples of three such questions: Why did Iago betray Othello? Is the universe infinite? What is art?

The assignments and activities in a unit explore components of the question. To engage in units that ask such questions, students must grapple with ambiguity and yet provide sound reasoning even if there is no "correct" answer. A 6th grade class engaged in a Socratic seminar was asked, "What is the proper role of the individual in response to a natural disaster?" To prepare for their seminar, they read excerpts from the Dalai Lama, John Donne, and a report on and map of the Deepwater Horizon oil spill. In turn, they wrote letters to students in the 4th and 5th grades addressing the question at the center of the assignment. Both the question and the theme of "individual responsibility to others" were addressed through texts, a worthwhile and interesting task for both the teacher and her students. The prompt read as follows: "What is the proper role of the individual in response to a 'disaster'? After reading various perspectives on individual responsibility and examining an interactive map of the 2010 Gulf Oil Disaster, write a letter to a younger child that addresses the question and support your position with evidence from the texts" (National Paideia Center for LDC).

> **Reflection Activity:** Fill in the blanks to complete a potential unit question. Consider your content and subject area.
> - Why_____?
> - How_____?
> - When_____?
> - What_____?

Moving From Novice to Expert

The historical apprenticeship system known as "guilds" offers an interesting way to create an environment of learning in a curriculum. In the guilds of the medieval and Renaissance eras, apprentices began their training as novices and strove to master basic techniques of the trade while being closely mentored. As they acquired confidence and skill, they took on more complicated tasks and responsibilities. Today, this approach is used in some businesses. For example, a major animation studio organizes its staffing in this way with new hires, or novices, starting out by drawing the basic shapes and figures used in the company's films until they can do them without thinking—that is, until they become "automatic." As new staff members acquire skill, they move to higher levels where they can design their own animations but in concordance with the basic techniques and style of the company.

You can plot a course using the apprenticeship model and distributing assignments along the continuum designated as novice, proficient, and advanced tasks. Here are some guidelines:

- *Novice:* Assignments that introduce students to new content and skills are novice demands. They may be low level, in that they are simple to execute or below grade level, but these lower demands should fade away as students acquire understanding and skills associated with higher levels of demand.
- *Proficient:* Assignments that challenge students with content and skills calibrated to grade level are "proficient." Assignments should be geared to this level for the majority of your instructional time; you can adjust upward as the year progresses. Assignments that demand performances and qualities that are deemed "proficient" are rigorous.
- *Advanced:* Assignments that ask students to stretch or manage more complex ideas and skills are what is called "high rigor." These advanced demands include qualities that are more nuanced or involve more difficult steps to solve. Nevertheless, they should be "doable" and still appropriate to students' grade or age level.

Adopt-a-Standard

One of the key features of the CCSS is the role of distributive responsibility for teaching literacy. This chapter concludes with a method that depends on district and school collaboration to increase the time and intensity of student engagement in foundational literacy and critical-thinking standards (you can include math as well). It's a strategy called "adopt-a-standard" that colleagues and I developed to ensure that literacy standards are taught across the curriculum. It involves a process of delegating specific standards to content courses and a commitment to teaching and assessing those standards. That is, priority standards are adopted by content-area teachers and are taught and assessed in their coursework. In states that assess only reading and math, adopt-a-standard relieves English and math teachers from being the only staff with the explicit responsibility to prepare students for state assessments and other high-stakes exams. Adopt-a-standard ensures that other teachers are helping students learn these essential learning skills. As important, if not more so, students receive multiple opportunities to acquire and practice these standards in different academic environments.

Why is this important? If the skills of learning to read, write, compute, apply logic, and develop other foundational skills are taught only during English and math class, students will not have sufficient time to internalize them to a level of fluency and adeptness necessary to participate in upper-level classes or in college or the workplace. Do the math: Students who are taught to write only in English class or taught math only in math class spend only a third of their day doing work that is aligned to the assessment system. On the other hand, if students are reading, writing, speaking and listening, computing, reading graphs, and applying statistics in other classes, they learn how to use literacy and math skills as they participate in other subjects (Crawford & Dougherty, 2004).

To make adopt-a-standard work requires staff to be deliberate. First, staff members meet and review ELA and math standards, with particular attention to assessed standards. Science, social studies, math, ELA, art, and PE staffs adopt one or more standards that fit well with their discipline and coursework and accept responsibility for teaching and assessing their choices. For example, a good fit for social studies is the research paper, or CCSS W2; music and arts might adopt reading nonfiction in the form of arts criticism and biographies.

A middle school staff in the Southwest whose student population was 100 percent Latino arrived at a plan that involved adopting standards and common assignments after finding that there was a wide range of interpretations among staff on how to transform standards into practice. They also realized that without intensive instruction in English and math, their students would not acquire the level of skill and understanding necessary to move into high school prepared for a faster-paced curriculum. Each term, teachers from each subject area designed units that included literacy standards, and some included math standards in computation, estimation, and statistics. As a result, their students moved from below proficient levels of achievement to above in just two years.

◆ ◆ ◆ ◆ ◆

Part 3

Beyond the Classroom

This section describes common assignments, or "Anchors," that can be taught across a school or a district. It then moves on to explain how to create ideal environments for developing and implementing assignments by paying attention to such factors as time, space, and available resources. Finally, it concludes with a discussion of how assignments can be used as a rich source of data about teaching and learning.

6

Anchor Assignments

To act is to anchor in the imminent future.

—Cioran, 2011

A powerful way to make assignments matter collectively in a school or a district—even a state—is to employ common assignments in order to "anchor" curriculum in effective practices aligned to priority standards. I refer to common assignments as "Anchors," a descriptive term connoting a curriculum grounded in common understandings and practices aligned to standards. Anchors transform standards into assignments and the practices involved in teaching them. A school or a district that decides to implement Anchors must value them as integral to the curriculum, not as an add-on or something to do to fill in literacy or math blocks.

The benefits of Anchors are many. Teachers benefit because they can share and build on their expertise and knowledge. Students benefit from Anchors because they receive targeted and intentional instruction throughout the school year in priority standards. Districts benefit because they can marshal resources and training in more efficient ways. Here's an example of a 9th grade Anchor assignment from the Portland, Oregon, Public Schools:

> From a literary text, select a literary element and write an
> essay that analyzes the element in the work. The selection
> of elements to be considered is character, setting, plot, theme,
> or tone.

Anchors have been used as a district strategy in a variety of ways to drive targeted instruction in priority standards and the core subjects. Portland, for example, assigned Anchors at grades 6 through 12 in each of the four core subjects each semester. Washington, D.C., Public Schools developed Anchors for each term in the core subjects in secondary schools on a voluntary basis. A Florida district has focused common assignments on reading at a single grade. Anchors can be distributed horizontally across a grade or vertically within a group of grades. Using Anchor prompts accompanied by increasingly more demanding rubrics can help teachers understand vertical alignment in concrete terms and, as a result, be better positioned to understand scaffolding and next-level demands.

The following two student samples were written in response to a common assignment taught in elementary and middle schools, the same prompt cited in Chapter 3 in which students wrote a review of a book they liked and explained why. We can easily see a progression in the use of language and context from the samples of a 2nd grader, who started out his first (ever) composition stating why he liked a movie, and an 8th grader. Here's the 2nd grader's response:

> My favorite movie is *Transformers*. I like it because it is cool. And these are the characters is Optimus prime and Bumblebee. . . . It is cool because Optimus prime have wings and can fly.

In comparison, the 8th grader uses her developing verbal skills to start with a reflection:

> All people have or will experience hardships, some more than others. These may break us, harden us, or embitter us. But, the true purpose of hardships is to learn from what has happened and become a stronger better person. All things happen for a reason, be it for good or bad. It takes courage and determination to find the real reasons for these hard points in life, but when you do, all will be worthwhile. This point is the backbone of the storyline in *Green Angel*. In a surreal

fairytale-like style, author Alice Hoffman tells the story of
15-year old Green, and the post-apocalyptic tale of how
she copes with the loss of her family and all she cares about
through a great fire. This book is very well written, and when
you pick it up, it will be hard to put down.

A Short History of Anchor Assignments

Performance assessments as a means to monitor student progress gained traction in the mid-1990s with the 1994 Title I reauthorization, which called for
a more accountable system, and they became a staple in districts by the next
decade, spurred on by the No Child Left Behind Act of 2001. In response,
districts designed monitoring systems based on common tests in reading and
math, called "benchmarks," given periodically during a school year. Benchmarks tend to be short, in-class tasks developed by district personnel and
purportedly aligned to assessed standards on state assessments. The data from
these benchmarks help districts gauge whether students are making progress
toward "proficient" or better scores on state assessments in order to meet
their Annual Yearly Progress (AYP) targets. Aldine, Texas, is an example of
a district that used benchmarks to successfully improve student achievement
(U.S. Department of Education, 2002–09).

According to a policy brief from the Assessment and Accountability
Comprehensive Center, "Benchmark assessments occupy a middle position
strategically located and administered outside daily classroom use but inside
the school and/or district curriculum" (Herman, Osmundson, & Deitel, 2010,
p. 2). In a benchmark system, teachers map backward to align instruction to
standards and assessments. However, there is no "standards police," so it's
inevitable that standards will be interpreted in very different ways (Sanders &
Rivers, 1996; Schmidt, McKnight, Cogan, Jakewerth, & Houng, 1999). That
is, Ms. B. may ask students to apply skills to solve problems, and Ms. C. may
ask them to practice skills day after day by filling out 20 problems on a ditto
sheet. Both teachers would tell you that they are "teaching the standards."

The idea and implementation of Anchor assignments evolved over
several years as an attempt to find ways to help teachers more accurately align

their work to standards. Along with other educators, I worked in two urban districts during the late 1990s and early 2000s to assist leadership in building a coherent professional development strategy. Vicki Phillips, who was then the superintendent in Lancaster, Pennsylvania, wanted to build a delivery system that drove instruction toward high expectations. She also wanted to be sure that all students, with few exceptions, received intentional instruction in essential content and skills. She brought me and other consultants to work with staff as a team to design a plan. The first year the team developed and implemented benchmark assessments. To support teachers, the district created a new position, an instructional facilitator at each school, whose main charge was to develop as a group a series of benchmarks in literacy and math and support teachers at their school sites. The benchmarks involved reading a passage and writing a short response about the passage. In math, students read a narrative problem, then showed their solution mathematically and explained their reasoning in writing. At the beginning of each term, teachers were given the assessed standards, usually no more than four, and generic rubrics but not the actual prompts or passages on the benchmarks.

Over time it became clear that the use of benchmark assessments was not producing the results the district wanted, either in student performance or in teacher instruction. Although we limited the skill sets by targeting only three or four standards, teachers struggled with interpreting these standards into everyday practice and were frustrated when they saw the prompts on the benchmark test. We heard comments complaining about the "secrecy" of the assessments and frustration over the "guesswork" in teaching to the test. These were the first years of the new accountability provisions under the Title I legislation of 1994, which required a standards-based system and evidence of student achievement in all groups. Teachers who had taught in a system that was more about compliance than meeting achievement goals struggled with the testing and transparency that occur in a benchmark system. The frustration and even anxiety this caused seemed to hinder the potential of the benchmarks to drive more intentional and effective instruction.

As an experiment, the district team rethought the benchmark assessments as assignments—that is, as taught tasks. We gave teachers grade-level common prompts and rubrics and told them to treat them as assignments. Professional development engaged teachers in mapping backward and making instructional choices that best fit the prompts and rubrics. They were asked to share the prompts and rubrics with students and to focus on teaching the content and skills. This approach shifted the focus on instruction rather than guesswork around alignment to standards and the benchmark assessments. As a result, the district, once facing a takeover by the state, met its AYP safe harbor targets. As I look back, I realize that by rethinking benchmark assessments as common assignments, the district developed the first version of Anchors.

Phillips took another position as superintendent in Portland, Oregon, in 2002. As before, she envisioned a strategy to ensure students received instruction in priority standards. We built on the lessons learned in Lancaster and this time focused on how to distribute responsibility for teaching literacy and math skills and practices across the curriculum (Wurtzel, 2007). The rationale was that literacy is the basic skill set necessary for participating fully in academic coursework and to perform on high-stakes assessments. Consequently, more time spent in coursework learning, practicing, and applying literacy skills would benefit students in any academic setting, whether in their subjects or taking a test (Crawford & Dougherty, 2004). A district team designed an Anchor delivery system and the environments and resources necessary to support teachers and students. (Chapter 7 discusses in more detail the second strategy involving rethinking how time and staffing arrangements can create classroom and professional environments to promote collaboration and intentional teaching.)

During the next two years, Portland implemented Anchors each term in grades 6 through 12, then added grades 3 through 5 in the third year. Throughout a school year, each core teacher taught at least one Anchor. For example, ELA teachers taught an Anchor in the first term that involved students in writing a character analysis. Social studies teachers taught an Anchor involving reading primary and secondary sources, and science teachers taught an Anchor involving a lab experiment. Coaches in ELL and special education designed Anchor lesson plans so that those students received appropriate instruction.

Because each Anchor shared common curricular themes or skills and they were vertically aligned, the district was able to provide coaching and professional development to support teachers more efficiently. For example, the first set of ELA Anchors for all grades involved writing a character analysis essay. This created a confluence of events in which professional development as well as classroom instruction coincided around this common skill set. When the year ended, the district discovered how powerful Anchor assignments can be: In a press release the district reported that students outpaced peers in the state in writing and math and improved scores for the first time in 10 years.

Beginning in 2009, the Gates Foundation supported a grant to develop a national literacy strategy that would transform the Common Core State Standards into practice. The resulting deliverable, the Literacy Design Collaborative, has been mentioned in previous chapters. I and five other team members put assignments at the center of this design. During the pilot, partner districts in six states taught two Anchors or common teaching tasks involving writing in response to reading around specific rhetorical modes. These common teaching tasks and modules were taught by ELA, social studies, and science teachers. Here's an example of an Anchor assignment for science:

> You work for a plastics company as a product designer. Design and conduct an experiment that measures the effect of at least two different conditions on the rate of several chemical reactions (e.g., high vs. low temperatures). After researching science articles on this topic, write a memo to your boss that explains how these conditions affect the rate of the reactions and how this information could help optimize the production of the company's new plastic cases.

Past experiences with Anchor assignments led to the design of the LDC framework, which involves templates of common assignments. Evaluations of the LDC framework as it has played out in classrooms are showing that LDC templates are a powerful mechanism for assisting teachers in aligning their work to the CCSS by changing teacher conversations, making staff aware of gaps in curriculum and instruction, and increasing collaboration. In interviews, administrators from two state agencies noted how the common tasks "exposed" needs and that "teachers are teaching differently and teaching for a purpose." A teacher in Georgia captured what other teachers said about the template design: "Teaching the LDC module has made me more thoughtful when planning lessons. I know I will do a better job next year, especially since I will have help from peers who will also be doing this."

Anchoring the Curriculum in Quality Assignments

Anchor assignments, if viewed as a central strategy of a well-planned policy for ensuring that students receive instruction in priority standards, serve that commitment in a number of ways:

- Anchor assignments ensure a focus on essential content and skills articulated in standards, assessments, and academic practices. Thinking critically, researching, reading closely, writing frequently, and solving problems are examples of academic practices students need to learn in order to function in any academic setting and are the Anchor skills in the Common Core State Standards.
- Anchor assignments ensure that most students, with few exceptions, receive instruction in essential standards. By ensuring participation, a school or district monitors equitable opportunity in the delivery of curriculum.
- Anchor assignments help to build consensus about what grade-level or subject-area rigor looks like in practice. They provide models of grade-level work and rigorous curriculum. In the process of creating Anchors and teaching them, teachers build consensus around what constitutes a quality assignment, how to score it, and how to teach the content and skills embedded in the task.
- Anchor assignments create opportunities for collecting data and feedback on learning-in-progress and the effectiveness of

instructional strategies or resources. To ensure that all students receive instruction in these key assignments, the school or district collects reports on student participation and progress to inform decisions about what supports are needed to improve achievement.

• Anchor assignments give professional development a common focus that allows teachers to learn from each other, to share strategies, and to improve their skills in teaching them. As well, the district has information that can assist it in making decisions about supports and resources. As a result, the dynamics of implementing common assignments create a professional community that solves instructional problems and focuses on what matters most—effective, meaningful curriculum and instruction.

Anchors as State Policy

For those states wanting to build a more coherent understanding of standards and outcomes, Anchors provide a policy venue for ensuring standards are taught and teachers provide substantive evidence of teaching those standards. The Education Trust, a nonprofit that advocates for students in public schools, has a long tradition of reporting data on state effectiveness in meeting learning goals and fulfilling the promise to ensure that students graduate with the educational experiences they need to succeed in college and the workplace. The organization continues to report the slow response by states to expect improvement for all schools and to collect better data to track progress (Education Trust, 2008). Anchors alone can't solve this challenge, but they can become a dynamic strategy for making those expectations clear and setting the stage for progress in achievement.

As it is, many districts rely on programs, such as Advanced Placement and International Baccalaureate, to provide an anchor in the secondary curriculum. Governor Gaston Caperton, as president of the College Board, acknowledged the potential of such programs to provide a common experience in the curriculum and as an "anchor" for increasing rigor (Caperton, 2006, p. 1). However, not all students have access to such courses. Anchor assignments, in contrast to programs or courses, offer a way to maintain rigor and increase students' participation in the learning that needs to be achieved if they are to manage college and a demanding workplace. Anchor assignments are a relatively inexpensive policy instrument to drive equity and access inside the educational system.

To date, a majority of states have adopted the Common Core State Standards. Kentucky, Pennsylvania, Colorado, and Georgia are rolling out the Literacy Design Collaborative modules and its counterpart in math, Transformation tasks, in order to build capacity around alignment to the CCSS. As a result, these states will have an invaluable bank of student work and instructional models on which to build for training and data purposes. Here's another example of an LDC Anchor, this time combining English language arts and science:

> **Task 11B (Informational or Explanatory/Definition)**
>
> After researching _____ (informational texts) on _____ (content), write a _____ (report or other product) that defines ___ and explains _____ (content). Support your discussion with evidence from your research.
>
> *Sample:* After researching <u>scientific articles</u> on <u>your organ system,</u> write a <u>report</u> that defines <u>"healthy"</u> and explains <u>the function and importance of your organ system.</u> Support your discussion with evidence from your research.

Developing a Plan to Make Anchors Matter

Whether you are a school, a district, or a state, you need a plan to implement Anchors. Your plan should consider a number of policy and practical factors and involve both school and district personnel in making decisions and developing documents. (Some of the resources you will need are more intangible, particularly those involving time, and these are discussed in Chapter 7.) The sections that follow here outline a prototype plan that you can follow or adjust to fit your needs and situations. The prototype plan involves a series of "choice points," or moments in the process when someone or some group needs to make decisions that affect the next steps and the overall implementation of the plan.

Phase 1: Plan Ahead

Start this phase well ahead of your launch date—if possible, the winter or spring term before the next school year in which you intend to implement Anchors. The larger your district or ambition, the sooner you need to start planning. You need time for thoughtful discussions about the purpose of the Anchors and more time to write and distribute assignments, to gather resources, and to accomplish a host of other tasks.

Anchors at a School. Administrators and a school team arrive at answers to these initial questions, with an input process to allow for feedback. Whole-staff conferencing follows to ensure all staff members understand the purpose, goals, and outcomes. Principals play a key leadership role in establishing the importance of the Anchors and their implementation.

Anchors Across a District. The district forms an Anchor team composed of representatives from participating schools and develops feedback loops to gather questions and comments on the plan as it unfolds. This might occur via staff meetings and an Anchor blog. It is important to the success of the Anchors in a district that the superintendent be apprised and take an active role in supporting the project.

The answers to each of the following Phase 1 questions, or "choice points," will determine next steps and resources.

Choice Points: Purpose, Goals, and Outcomes

1. What do you want to accomplish overall? Example: Create environments in which core and elective teachers share responsibility for instructing students in assessed standards involving critical thinking, reading, writing, and basic math skills.

2. What are your goals? Example: To increase the time and intensity of instruction students receive in skills aligned to the Common Core ELA Standards.

3. What are your outcomes? Example: To increase the amount of reading and writing that occurs in all core coursework by 30 percent and in electives by 15 percent. To increase the amount of mathematical skills applied in core coursework by 15 percent.

4. What is the accountability for teaching the Anchors? A policy needs to be developed that makes clear if the teaching of Anchors is required or voluntary.

This sample passage from a large urban district's plan lays out its overall strategy:

> The Office of Curriculum and Instruction will work closely with representatives from schools to develop strategies and tools to:
>
> - Use the context of the Anchor assignments to improve teaching skills in reading, writing, and critical thinking;
> - Understand a method for aligning assignments to the Common Core Standards for ELA and Literacy in History/Social Studies, Science, and Technical Subjects in view of adoption next year;
> - Involve staff in a process of formative assessment— using the desired outcomes of taught assignments to inform next-step instruction;
> - Create a bank of Anchors around key standards, concepts, and topics relevant to the four core content areas of ELA, mathematics, science, and social studies.

Answers to Phase 1 questions should be made available to all participants as well as students and their parents. The kinds of assignments parents will see their students engage in may be unfamiliar, especially in schools where reading, writing, and language usage are not commonly applied in classwork outside of English language arts. A brief discussion or pamphlet describing Anchors and their role in the curriculum is good community policy.

Reflection Activity: What would be your goal in implementing Anchors? What standards would you target? What kinds of challenges (for example, problem-based learning, academic writing) would you want to engage students in?

Phase 2: Set the Stage

Once consensus has been reached on the purpose, goals, and outcomes for the Anchors, you decide on the logistics that set the stage for implementation. This involves putting in place the practical activities that will make the processes of managing, distributing, teaching, gathering, scoring, and analyzing Anchors go smoothly.

Choice Points: Get Ready, Get Set . . .

1. How many Anchors, and in what courses and grades? Answers to this question start with an analysis of the school or district data. The strategic way of thinking is to target the areas where students need the most support to perform well on assessments and to participate in next-level coursework. For example, if students are weak in identifying main ideas and supporting details in texts, Anchors that target those skills can be taught in ELA, social studies, and science. If students are weak at estimating in math, Anchors that target that skill can be reinforced in math, science, and social studies.

One way to start is to consider a simple schedule involving two core subjects teaching an Anchor each term or semester; another approach is to expand the schedule to allow for teaching one Anchor per term in the four core areas. Whatever schedule you develop should have a rationale and be linked to targeting weaknesses in student performances or to skills and content that need more attention in the curriculum.

2. Who manages the Anchor project? An Anchor project requires coordination and management and is best served by appointing a position in each school to manage the project. This person should keep everyone involved up to date and report to the principal. For example, in Lancaster, the superintendent created the role of instructional facilitator at each school and a district point person. In another district, literacy and math coaches assumed this responsibility.

3. Who develops the Anchors, and how does this happen? Writing the Anchors should be a team effort, with teachers, coaches, and administrators participating. This approach gives the Anchor development process a two-pronged purpose: to get a variety of experts in the room and to build collaboration and teamwork. An urban superintendent, on visiting one such session, told a colleague that she had witnessed the best professional development she'd ever seen. What she saw was a group of teachers and coaches engaged in professional dialogue, grappling with the elements of content, skill, and context to write a prompt (see Chapter 3). The act of writing an Anchor is powerful professional development because it asks participants to consider the curriculum as a whole, the standards, and their respective meaning in practice.

4. *How will the Anchors be distributed and collected after each cycle?* Whether you are a school or a district, the Anchors should be analyzed and reported as feedback in a variety of forms. A system for collecting scores and student work needs to be designed so that it isn't cumbersome or time-consuming.

5. *What training and resources will teachers need?* The quick answer to this is "time." Teachers need time to understand the instructional components of the Anchor in order to teach, score, and analyze the results. You may have to come back to this question for more specifics once the Anchor has been written. However, you should anticipate the following:

- Periodic training at the start of each cycle.
- School or district professional development days for scoring and reporting feedback on the Anchors.
- Common planning time so that teachers can meet and discuss the progress of the Anchor work on a weekly or biweekly basis. Chapter 7 discusses ways to create an environment that supports Anchors by rethinking schedules and staffing interactions to increase opportunities for collaboration necessary for teaching and scoring an Anchor.
- Resources, such as class sets of books, labs, computer use, and software programs. For example, one district found that there were no class sets of a title, so teaching an Anchor based on a common text was impossible. They were able, however, to find free short stories online. Another district has found that a software program that coaches students through the composing

process on writing Anchors helped both the students and teachers manage the time and effort multiple revisions require. (See Appendix E for a list of resources that may be helpful.)

Figure 6.1 shows a sample calendar from an urban district for Phase 2 of an Anchor project.

Figure 6.1	
Sample Calendar for Anchor Project, Phase 2	
Date	**Tasks**
April	1—Meet with school principals and finalize agreement (scope of work, roles, responsibilities, potential for performance reviews)
	2—Meet with Anchor Team (school-based instructional coaches and consultants) to determine grade levels for A1 Anchors and begin writing for A1 Anchor bank
May	1—Finalize bank of A1 Anchors
	2—Send out information packet to schools with schedules and guidelines
	3—Distribute A1 Anchors
	4—Develop and prepare for August training

Reflection Activity: What would you need to do in your school or district to implement Anchors? Consider schedules, resources, policies, and staff responsibilities.

Phase 3: Implement Anchors

Following is a list of questions to guide your planning and thinking about what steps you should take to create the supports and infrastructures that make Anchor assignments possible.

Choice Points: Support and Implementation

1. *What supports do teachers need, and in what form?* There is no pat answer or formula for this question. However, if the content and the skill

set embedded in the Anchors are complex (comparing a number of factors, for example), unfamiliar, or require students to perform multiple steps, then teachers need support to varying degrees. Anchors give a particular focus to professional development, which should be closely linked to the Anchors' content and the demands and qualities embedded in the prompt and rubric (see Chapter 3). You can anticipate that teachers will need support in understanding the purpose of an Anchor prompt and in being clear on what their expectations are. They may need coaching in specific instructional skills, such as how to break an assignment down into incremental steps and choosing instructional strategies specific to the assignment. Unlike a system in which teachers are on their own, Anchors make it possible for a more targeted professional development plan. As well, because teachers are solving the same instructional challenges, they can solve many of them together. Figure 6.2 shows a sample calendar from an urban district for the first part of Phase 3.

Reflection Activity: What professional development would you (teacher or administrator) and your staff need to implement Anchors?

Figure 6.2	
Sample Calendar for Anchor Project, Phase 3 (Part 1)	
Date	**Tasks**
August	1—One-day training: teachers @ model schools
	2—Meet with Anchor Team to begin writing A2 Anchors for Anchor Curriculum
	3—School visits by Anchor Team and coach teams

   2. What happens if a teacher doesn't teach an Anchor to designated students? Only a district can address this policy question since it involves a number of local factors. The guiding principle involves "opportunity to learn." Struggling and inexperienced students, English Langauge Learners students, and special education students should not be excluded, since accommodations can be made in most cases. For example, all students can participate in an Anchor that asks them to construct a model of an arc or to write a report on World War II. Some students may need more intervention or reading materials leveled so that they can access information. When scoring, student names should be taken off papers to avoid making judgments based on such labels.

3. How does staff score student work? The process used in scoring Anchors is the same as the process described in Chapter 3, except at scale. You can make this process more interesting if teachers and administrators score in teams or with other schools and grades. In one such session, middle school science teachers learned that high school teachers were adamant about a lab report with elements that the middle school teachers were not teaching, particularly the difference between a result and a conclusion. Their conversation during scoring made it possible for the middle school staff to address these distinctions in their courses and better prepare students for high school science. Figure 6.3 shows a sample calendar from an urban district for the remainder of Phase 3.

Figure 6.3	
Sample Calendar for Anchor Project, Phase 3 (Part 2)	
Date	**Tasks**
November	1—Finalize bank of A2 Anchors
	2—Determine which Anchors to field-test at model schools for A2
	3—Distribute A2 Anchors for field testing (A3 begins January 24 and ends March 25)
	4—Prepare for February training
	5—A1 Anchors due
	6—Scoring camp[1] (Anchor Team and participating teachers)
	7—Meet with Anchor Team to begin writing A3 Anchors for Anchor Curriculum

[1] Scoring camp is a session in which instructional coaches rescore sample student work on the Anchors. This session is modeled and should be repeated at the school level to help teachers gauge their scoring against the samples.

Phase 4: Feedback Loop

To provide teachers with useful feedback, the district or school collects data and presents them in formats that allow for analyses about effectiveness of the Anchor, effectiveness of instructional choices, and student progress. These methods are discussed in more detail in Chapter 8.

Choice Points: Data as Feedback

1. How do teachers give useful feedback to students? Students need feedback during the process of working on a product as well as after the product is scored. If assignments are broken down into smaller tasks, teachers can provide feedback as students complete the product. For example, a science teacher might give students step-by-step guidelines for a lab experiment and check off each step when students adequately or accurately complete it. This type of monitoring prevents students from going off-track.

2. How does the school or district use the scoring data so that they improve student performance and instructional effectiveness? The data that come back from Anchors are revealing about what students and teachers need to do to improve student performance on priority learning goals and to be prepared to take on increasingly difficult academic challenges. At the district level, data reports should analyze whole-class performances first. At the school, teachers can analyze individual or group performances. Reports should target overall outcomes as well as those smaller issues involving content and skills that affect student learning. Because one of the goals of Anchors is to ensure that students receive instruction in priority content and skills, it is important to collect participation data. Teachers should be given multiple opportunities to analyze data, as they provide them with valuable information to make decisions about, or corrections to, their coursework plans. Figure 6.4 shows a sample calendar for Phase 4.

Reflection Activity: What data would help teachers improve their instructional choices?

Figure 6.4

Sample Calendar for Anchor Project, Phase 4

Date	Tasks
June	1—One-day training (consultants, teachers @ model schools)
	2—A4 Anchors due
	3—Scoring camp (Anchor Team and participating teachers)
	4—Meet with Anchor Team to finalize bank of A1 Anchors; discuss lessons learned for Anchors 2010–11
	5—School visits by Anchor Team
	6—Off-site lesson planning, Anchor writing
July	1—Meet with model school principals, discuss: Lessons learned for Anchors 2010–11 Potential for full adoption in model schools for SY 2011–12
	2—Prepare final report

Challenges to Making Anchors Matter

In reality, any activity, much less one that involves change, implemented at scale has its challenges—even barriers—to overcome if it is to be successful. Education has a long history and large body of research attempting to answer the question of why change in education is so hard to manage and sustain. Michael Fullan (2007), who has long contemplated this question, reminds us that "solving complex problems on a continuous basis is enormously difficult because of the sheer number of factors at play" (p. 115). Accordingly, you can anticipate that implementing Anchors in an effort to bring coherence to a school or a district will face challenges. Some of these are specific to Anchors, and others are deeply embedded in the school culture. Nevertheless, the benefits outweigh these challenges because Anchors have the potential to redefine for the better how teachers teach and how they work together. Fullan reminds us that change is not inevitably doomed if educators are deliberate and have a plan. One teacher commenting to me on his experience with teaching an Anchor reflected, "I was against the Anchor at first, but I've changed my mind. I definitely saw improvement in student work."

Transparency

In school reform, educators and researchers generally view transparency as a good thing. However, when transparency causes teacher work to be exposed to others, whether within a small group of colleagues or the larger community, people can find this exposure uncomfortable or even react with suspicion. Because Anchors are taught and scored collaboratively and feedback is analyzed collaboratively, Anchors make transparent what teachers do in the classroom. For some teachers who have taught in self-contained classrooms for many years, putting their work "out there" to be discussed and analyzed can be intimidating and difficult.

In our work with districts implementing Anchors, experienced teachers tended to be more cautious, and new teachers were more willing to put their work in the middle of a team meeting or to ask for help early on in the project. In most cases, teachers found the conversations around the work they shared in common stimulating. This challenge can become productive when conversations around Anchors involve problem solving and are professionally pertinent. To ensure this happens, facilitators need training in monitoring professional dialogue.

Project managers and administrators participating in the Literacy Design Collaborative reported that teachers' conversations while developing the prompts were focused and intense. They shared their knowledge of content and instructional skills in order to craft teaching tasks (assignment prompts) and to create plans. Likewise, during scoring sessions in which teachers worked in small groups, teachers analyzed which instructional choices were effective and which were not, building a broader understanding of instructional efficacy. They used this feedback to reflect and to plan for the next teaching cycle. "I would do it differently next time," wrote one middle school teacher. "As I progressed through this unit, I realized that three weeks was not enough to teach students everything they needed to know in order to write an essay that would be proficient according to all areas of the final rubric."

Time

Having enough time to teach and learn is a constant challenge, and in my experience, this is the most frequently mentioned barrier to teaching assignments effectively. In *Prisoners of Time*, a report published almost two decades ago, the lack of time to teach—including time to think, plan, and implement instruction deeply—is discussed as a barrier to quality instruction (National Education Commission on Time and Learning, 1994). The Common Core State Standards, with their emphasis on text complexity and analysis, among other skills, demand teaching that is thoughtful and persistent. Coverage is not the goal here, and these are not standards teachers can just check off as they deliver the curriculum. Leadership and curriculum developers must decide how to create the optimal schedules for instruction and professional development so that teaching and learning are possible (Crawford & Dougherty, 2004). Districts need to review the number and purpose of the programs and "must do" dictates that take up teacher and administrative time but may not produce much in the way of student gains. One large urban district did an audit only to find that it had more than 200 programs operating in schools. The district proceeded to eliminate most of them in an attempt to clear the way for more responsive teaching.

Anchors depend on the productive use of time. For one, collaboration is not going to happen if the schedule does not include weekly planning time. Building consensus around the meaning of rubrics is not going to happen if teachers can't score in teams throughout the year. The strategic use of time is a necessity if teachers are to work through the Anchors together, sharing responsibilities for teaching and scoring. Students need time to learn, too. They need time to succeed as well as fail, to revise, to discuss, to grapple with complex ideas. They need time to conference with their teachers to ensure they are getting feedback on their progress on assignments. Chapter 7 discusses methods for creating environments that support intentional teaching, and time is a key element in these environments.

Resources

Lack of resources also poses challenges and can impede intentional teaching of assignments. Are there enough books on an Anchor topic? Are there resources for students to take a field trip, for example, to the local planetarium to enliven instruction around stars? Do all students have access to computers to write, compute, or develop presentations? Resources are necessary for teachers, too; they may need coaches and other expertise to help them learn skills they don't have or need to improve. Teachers and students may need technologies and materials that help them address a range of abilities.

Reflection Activity: From your perspective, as a teacher leader or administrator, what challenges might you anticipate, and what can you do to be prepared to resolve them?

Building Professional Community

A good topic to end this chapter with is not the challenges but the benefits. The most important dynamic resulting from implementing Anchors we experienced as we worked with staffs over the past decade is a dynamic built on professional relationships. When teachers and administrators come together to address work that matters in their classrooms, they form professional communities. Astuto defines a professional community as one "in which the teachers in a school and its administrators continuously seek and share learning and then act on what they learn. The goal of their actions is to enhance their effectiveness as professionals so that students benefit. This arrangement has also been termed communities of continuous inquiry and improvement" (SEDL, 1997). Professional communities are powerful venues for school change and improvement. SEDL, a Texas-based research organization, recommends that "persons at all levels of the educational system concerned about school improvement—state department personnel, intermediate service agency staff, district and campus administrators, teacher leaders, key parents and local school community members"—should see professional communities as a viable way of creating environments that are professional, taking on the everyday and larger challenges of running a school system.

When school or district staff are involved in common activities with common goals, people rise to the occasion and help each other. An assistant superintendent of a small urban district who joined her teachers throughout the process of writing and planning LDC Anchors recounted her experience as one in which she and her teachers came to "understand" each other and have conversations they never would have had without the "common" in common assignments. She explained to me that she was able to work with them to solve instructional problems, such as how to teach students not to plagiarize when writing a research paper. In her role as an administrator she gained firsthand knowledge about what training and resources teachers needed to teach rigorous assignments. Another educator in charge of a multidistrict effort had a similar experience. She discovered that teachers at one of her middle schools did not have enough books to teach all 7th grade students from the same book. She found the money to order enough copies so that every student had one. Such interactions are invaluable experiences that cannot happen when teachers are on their own to write and teach assignments. Chapter 7 describes ways in which educators can create environments that make teaching assignments with depth and understanding possible.

◆ ◆ ◆ ◆ ◆

7

Environments That
Make Assignments Matter

Human beings have an innate inner drive to be autonomous,
self-determined, and connected to one another. And when that
drive is liberated, people achieve more and live richer lives.

—Pink, 2009, p. 71

Any environment affects how people interact. In a classroom, the environment affects how teachers and students connect with ideas and each other.
Because high-rigor assignments require time, energy, and collaboration
from teachers and students, environments play a critical role in ensuring
that assignments become staples of the curriculum and are taught intentionally. Many an excellent teacher has taught students who went on to become
productive citizens using only a blackboard, chalk, and a pile of textbooks.
But there are so many more possibilities today for creating environments
supportive of teaching and learning. There is no need for students to sit all
day in classrooms relying heavily on teacher-talk, worksheets, rows of desks,
and bulletin boards. Technology and other interactive experiences offer end-
less possibilities to engage everyone—teachers, students, even parents and
visitors—in the intellectual life of ideas. Environments that allow teachers
to teach assignments and, in doing so, employ a wide array of instructional
experiences in and outside of the classroom are places where students can
become "autonomous, self-determined, and connected to one another." Such
a classroom is an exciting place to be.

In Ms. T.'s classroom there is time to discuss ideas and to read and write about them. There are spaces and resources to conduct experiments and to explore how things work. Students often interview experts in the community and communicate electronically on a topic with national experts. Ms. T. strives to motivate her students by designing lessons that involve intellectual and social interactions and the intrigue of problems to be solved. Ms. T. has time to confer with other teachers and to solve instructional challenges, to design assignments, to score, and to give students feedback. She has both indoor and outdoor spaces to manage the learning experience. Ms. T. has an optimal environment in which she can make teaching assignments not only possible but rewarding. Her environment is a classroom that could be in elementary or secondary schools.

Teachers who have crafted assignments and their lesson plans using the seven-step process outlined in this book realize that teaching an assignment is not about checking off a "just do it" list. Teaching assignments, particularly Anchor assignments, brings into relief the need for thoughtfully constructed environments because challenging assignments depend on infrastructures that allow teachers and students to interact with each other and to use technologies that enhance their learning. Teaching assignments demands time and space to accomplish tasks; but most important, such teaching needs time and space to *think*, and thinking is hard work. Teachers need time and space to plan and teach, to score, and to provide feedback, often with colleagues. Students also need time and space to think, to discuss, and to do things— read, write, compute, experiment, explore—over and over, if necessary, in order to get it right. (Remember, an assignment is taught. It is not "given" or "assigned"; nor is it a summative assessment.) School- and district-level administrators and other educators can support teachers by understanding the demands involved in crafting and delivering quality assignments and making policies that recognize and honor their efforts.

This chapter explores a few critical environmental factors—time, space, resources—that influence how assignments are taught, using a case-study approach to help convey what infrastructures make teaching and learning a richer experience. I start with *time*, particularly the school schedule, because it is the most frequently cited environmental factor that teachers mention in our discussions about how to implement assignments. That frequency is not surprising, since time influences how people inside a school interact with each other and approach learning and teaching. *Space* is an often forgotten element of the school environment, but one that also profoundly affects people in an educational community. Teachers need spaces that will allow them to deepen the experiences that can make an assignment more substantive and meaningful—a science lab for an experiment or a room to hold seminars, for example. They need spaces where they can work on their own and spaces for collaboration. Material *resources*, including media and technology, are imperative if teachers are to accomplish goals and provide interesting learning experiences—in particular, a variety of texts that allow students to engage in challenging syntax and ideas as described in the Common Core State Standards (2001, p. 57).

Administrators can contribute to an effective environment by establishing supportive policies, particularly those that encourage rather than discourage innovation and flexibility. With time, space, resources, and supportive policies, teachers have what they need to implement an assignment-rich curriculum. When you take on the environment to make it more adaptable to assignment teaching, you'll find that a ripple effect occurs that affects more than assignments. One automatic benefit is increased communication and collaboration.

Take, for example, Dan and Chad, two social studies teachers who teach in the same middle school but had never really talked or worked together. Their school participated in an LDC Anchor assignment, and in the process Dan and Chad collaborated on every aspect of the assignment and instruction. They found this collaboration to be so helpful that they continued their coteaching on three more assignments. The results noted in a report undertaken by a research group for the Gates Foundation cited these and other teachers who commented that their students "can do more than we had been asking them to do" (Research for Action, 2011).

When possible and appropriate, an assignment can take on an interesting dimension when you coteach, working in partnership with other subject-area teachers who bring specific expertise to the assignment. Imagine art and history teachers or physical education and science teachers collaborating on an assignment. In each case, students would come to understand the interrelatedness of knowledge fields and how these connections often lead to new ideas and practices.

Case Study #1: Time Is of the Essence

Our current operating system has become far less compatible with, and at times downright antagonistic to: how we organize what we do; how we think about what we do; and how we do what we do.

—Pink, 2009, p. 20

Needless to say, "time" is a necessity often cited by teachers and probably the most challenging obstacle to teaching assignments. An important report published almost two decades ago, *Prisoners of Time*, starts off with the observation that "learning in America is a prisoner of time" (National Education Commission on Time and Learning, 1994, p. 7). The report goes on to lay out a series of time-related issues that plague the school day, impeding collaboration, time on task, and other necessary duties that make teaching and learning possible. Time that is not used well is, of course, lost opportunity. However, time that is well planned and relevant to instructional goals pays off in results. Time to craft and deliver assignments requires environments that support your efforts to think, to plan, to collaborate, to instruct, to provide feedback, and to score. If you add up the hours spent before, during, and after school on school-related work, you will find that teachers spend considerably more than the workplace average of 40 hours a week. Typically, secondary teachers work some 65 hours a week, teaching six classes a day, and elementary teachers spend about the same amount of time with fewer students but with the same pressures and responsibilities. It is not unusual to find middle and high school teachers with 80 or more students, even 150 or more. Every page of student work to review or score adds more minutes to this calculation (Crawford & Dougherty, 2004).

Kathy, a high school history teacher in Oregon, had 205 students enrolled in her six classes, which included Advanced Placement coursework as well as students with special needs and students reading below grade level. Nevertheless, Kathy taught six rigorous LDC assignments in which students researched a period of history and a relevant topic and wrote essays. She also collected short intermediary tasks (notes, bibliographies, drafts) that led to completion of student essays. A calculation revealed that Kathy collected more than 2,000 student pages for one assignment and 6,000 pages for all six assignments. Why would a teacher take on so much work? Kathy reported that her students, by engaging in these reading and writing assignments, did better on the end-of-course exam than students in other classes who did not engage in assignments. This result has convinced her colleagues in her department to try teaching assignments next year.

Reflection Activity: What can be done to help Kathy manage these assignments without burnout? What could you and your colleagues do to create a better schedule, allowing more time for you to collaborate on assignments?

Clearly, Kathy could use some help if she and her colleagues are to sustain teaching assignments that involve an emphasis on a range of literacy practices. Two changes in Kathy's environment would make a difference in her capacity to include assignments in her coursework and have the time she needs for instruction, scoring, preparing, and—not to be forgotten—thinking. They are (1) teaching Anchor assignments by department and (2) coteaching with another teacher.

Teaching Anchor Assignments by Department

Using common assignments, Kathy and her department colleagues can teach common skill sets in historical thinking, research, planning, and writing, all while teaching content relevant to each course. This would enable the group to share instructional strategies and provide feedback when scoring final papers. Working together on an assignment also takes away the sense of isolation that so many teachers feel as they struggle to deliver high-quality instruction.

This scenario requires common planning time and affects how schedules are constructed to allow for weekly meetings, at best, for at least a period. Quick meetings at lunch just won't create the necessary time and ambience for working together. To create a schedule that allows for frequent planning involves administration and even district understanding and support, since schedules are key to any school infrastructure. School redesign expert Marilyn Crawford has developed a process for designing master schedules that optimize the use of time and other resources in support of instruction. Among other things, she has helped schools construct schedules that give teachers a range of options for collaborating and coteaching. For example, she has reconstructed schedules to give an entire faculty two hours to a half-day each week. One high school designed a schedule allotting a full day every two weeks for engaging in the practices that make teaching high-quality assignments possible—sharing expertise, scoring, and collecting formative data. Her work evolved out of the challenge of helping districts redesign secondary schools around performance goals and college readiness for all.

Finding time and energy for assignments involving reading, writing, speaking, and listening may not be possible in a traditional schedule. The Common Core State Standards for ELA demand that students engage in literacy practices throughout the day and school year in the core areas. Consequently, time to do this is a necessary factor in aligning teaching and learning to these standards. They ask for a level of engagement in literacy practices that demand time, for example, to read "closely," to write "short research projects," to cite "textual evidence," to "participate in a range of conversations," and to read "independently" (see the CCSS Anchor Standards). These are just some examples of the activities students must engage in if they are to meet expectations embedded in the CCSS. Where literacy is practiced, time is a necessary condition to practice its skills and applications well.

Coteaching

If Kathy and an English teacher colleague coteach, they can "divide and conquer." In this scenario, Kathy and her colleague Irene share responsibilities for teaching content and literacy skills during a two-hour block rather than two 55-minute periods. In this scenario, a number of shared teaching practices happen. For one, Kathy teaches content and supports Irene's work on literacy skills, such as those necessary for reading historical documents. Irene teaches literary or other texts that relate to the assignment, teaching students how to approach and read different kinds of texts and to extract textual evidence. She also manages the writing process of the assignment, with Kathy ensuring that students have the content and rhetorical skills required in the assignment. In this scenario, they plan each week how to group students in a schedule that supports the assignment.

Coteaching helps each teacher better manage an assignment from beginning to end because they have two people and two hours rather than teaching separately in isolated classrooms for 55-minute periods. Also, this arrangement enables them to adjust class routines, group students for specific reasons, and share instructional responsibilities to meet students' needs. Because their classrooms are side by side, students can easily move from classroom to classroom, regroup, and work according to a daily plan.

For example, consider that Kathy and Irene are teaching an assignment involving reading, research, and writing an essay on the American Revolution. Kathy needs Wednesday and Thursday to complete the research step in the assignment. She and Irene assign students to each other's classrooms according to the feedback about students' strengths and support needs that they culled from a pre-test and previous assignments. Kathy keeps one group for two days, while Irene works with students on planning an essay and note-taking skills, which prepare students for the research step. Throughout the assignment, these two coteachers plan how to best move students through each step of the assignment. In this arrangement, Kathy shares those 2,000 sheets of paper with another teacher, and she has backup to help decide what feedback and coaching are necessary at each step of the teaching process. This paired arrangement makes teaching assignments collaborative and more doable.

Creating the environment for paired teaching requires attention to curriculum as well as schedule and teaching assignments. This challenge was presented to Marilyn Crawford and me a few years ago at a middle school with an enrollment of 4,800 students and a year-round calendar. We worked with the administrative staff and teachers, including union representatives, to create an environment that better positioned teachers to teach extended lessons, with an emphasis on assignments involving literacy in English language arts and social studies. It was crucial that students in this all-minority school gain as much instruction and practice on literacy skills as possible in order to be prepared for the pace and load of high school coursework. Crawford designed a schedule extending teaching time over two periods by pairing teachers and placing them in adjoining classrooms. The principal held a fiesta at the school on a Saturday while parents helped move teachers to their new classrooms. In this paired setting, collaboration was possible, and each teacher could take responsibility for teaching content and skills. Meanwhile, I worked with staff to design course maps that ensured that what happened in those longer periods involved a coherent approach to teaching literacy practices, with a focus on writing in response to reading.

Case Study #2: Making Room for Assignments

"Spaces themselves are agents for change. Changed spaces will change practice" (Joint Information System Committee, 2006, p. 30). The role of space in creating environments friendly to teaching in general is an important factor, but particularly when teaching assignments. Marzano points out that "the physical setting of the classroom conveys a strong message regarding a teacher's approach to managing instruction and learning" (2007, p. 121). Even when teaching the "old-fashioned way" with books, blackboards, and desks, how we use space can affect how we employ assignments and get results. Drake, a first-year teacher, exemplifies in the following case study how his use, and nonuse, of space detracted from his attempts to teach his students an assignment involving percentages.

Drake was clearly having trouble keeping his 15 middle school students' attention while he explained how to compute percentages for an assignment in which students had to report on a survey. He had a large room with windows and natural light and an expanse of open space. His students sat in three rows close to the front near the blackboard and only paces away from both doors to the hallway. One row was empty because six students were absent, not an unusual number for his classes or his school. A clock hung over one door, steadily ticking away each second, in clear view of the students. The doors had glass panels, allowing students to see anyone passing by. Two students were trying valiantly to pay attention, but one of their peers kept interrupting. Three students in the back seats were passing notes, and the quiet students kept looking at the clock. A couple of times, students in the hallway waved at the class through the transparent door windows; one passerby pressed her nose against the glass and made faces. This caused the class to turn away from Drake and lose attention. The student who had been acting out from the beginning of class jumped up as if to let the person at the door in and loudly announced he was doing so. Since he was sitting near the door, it was easy for him to get to it, feigning his "helpfulness." When Drake admonished him to "pay attention or else," this student settled down for a few minutes, then continued to find ways to not pay attention. All in all, Drake and some of his students spent only a few minutes of their period on task. A few spent no time on task.

Drake asked a colleague to observe and to note specifically how he might better use his space to manage student behaviors. His colleague listed the following ways Drake might use the physical space to better advantage:

- Use the large space in the classroom to create multiple learning experiences directed toward solving the assignment's problem rather than teaching computational steps on the easel, lecture style.

- Create work centers with manipulatives and other aides students can use if they need them to work through aspects of the assignment.
- Use the large room to organize small work groups with sufficient elbow room and distance between groups to avoid interactions that are off-task.
- When working with the whole group, have students sit in a semi-circle around the board or easel and place this setting away from the doors. This enables teacher–student eye contact at all times and puts students at an equal distance from the teacher, unlike rows, which create too much distance between the teacher and some students.
- Move the clock out of sight, and cover the doors with a paper poster.

Reflection Activity: What else might Drake have done with his physical environment to help his students focus? How could "new media" help Drake construct a more inviting and supportive environment?

Physical space, how it is designed and used, is often overlooked as an environmental element that affects the dynamic of the classroom. For example, many teachers in our LDC project cited the "hassle" of getting their students frequent access to computers as a deterrent to teaching writing. When teachers have access to space and use it purposefully, they create opportunities for a greater range of activities for students to experience.

Space is needed for discussions, projects, and conferencing—the learning activities that support the teaching of assignments. At the very least, teaching assignments requires space for small-group as well as individual work, space for computer work, and quiet spaces to read. If teachers want to engage students in more complex learning experiences, such as science labs, interviews, mock trials, or hands-on projects, they clearly need elbow room and the room to talk and do things. Challenging and interesting assignments thrive on a variety of activities. Teachers can address complex ideas and skill sets through different lenses, creating intellectual and practical learning opportunities. Needless to say, as new media become an integral part of the classroom environment, space becomes even more important, affecting learning and teaching in new ways. But even some of the old approaches can have a large impact on learning, as the following anecdote illustrates.

As a new teacher with 30 2nd grade students in a "no walls" classroom environment, I experienced not only how space can affect teaching but also how the use of space can change how you teach. I had placed a large round table in my classroom area to create a space for conversation. The circular table created a practical and symbolic center for our classroom for interactions throughout the day. The table became a safe and quiet space for conferencing and small-group discussions about books and topics. It became the intellectual center of the classroom dynamic. One day an administrator decided that the round table must go, preferring that I keep students in rows and at their desks. The absence of that simple round table changed the entire dynamic of the learning environment—and not for the better.

The experience of a veteran principal who took over a failing elementary school attended by low-income students provides another example of the importance of space. The principal made her first move to "rehab" the school by creating new spaces. Before students arrived she redesigned a playground area with colorful new slides and play equipment and filled a music room with shiny new instruments. When students arrived to meet the new principal, they felt as if they were in a new school. These spaces were not just for effect. These were spaces where students learned things such as the self-discipline of attending to a musical instrument and the responsibilities of playing fairly. After two years, this school became a model for educational attainment and earned support from the larger community. It wasn't long before this Title I school had a waiting list of students from all over the city.

Attention to physical space can also create room for intellectual and academic activities by carving out spaces where ideas can thrive in a classroom—the kind of environment that's necessary for challenging assignments. A cramped classroom without room to move around curtails participation in a number of ways. Students become antsy or apathetic after sitting hour on hour at their desks. They give up on participating in discussions or act out just to cut through their boredom. Teaching is affected, too, when teachers are forced to stay in front of the classroom. In contrast, classrooms or schools that have spaces to hold discussions, work on projects, work in small and large groups, and use technology enrich and enable learning and teaching.

Discussion is so critical for developing intellectually active learners that some schools have created defined spaces in classrooms and schools where these conversations can happen frequently. In classrooms with enough room for discussions without distractions, students engage in meaningful discourse, as in Amy's and Melissa's classrooms in their respective middle schools. Each week, they pull students into a circle and conduct Paideia seminars. Seminar is their way of building discourse and intellectual experiences into their assignment lesson plans. Inside that circle, students engage in meaningful talk to understand texts in a deeper way than is possible by "just reading" them. They use this understanding to develop their thinking in their written assignments. That circle creates a sense of equity and cooperation in ways that rows of desks cannot. In a circle, students respond to questions and explore their responses together as equals. Each contributes in some way, applying literacy practices in speaking, listening, sometimes viewing, and questioning. In seminar, the teacher does not cue students or provide answers or opinions (Billings & Roberts, 2012).

Another important and necessary environment for learning is space for doing things—hands-on and active experiences. These are spaces where the learning embedded in assignments can thrive and grow, maybe literally. The Edible Schoolyard in Berkeley uses outside and inside spaces to provide experiential learning as part of the instructional program. I conducted a workshop for teachers and community members from around the country in which they learned the seven steps for crafting an assignment to create tasks involving gardens and food science. These assignments not only were fun to do but also demanded knowledge of science as well as practical skills to accomplish them. Schools that have outdoor spaces have wonderful opportunities to create assignments in science and other subjects.

The good news is that newer and renovated schools are incorporating space for discussion and activities in their design. A high school on the West Coast employs a bold design that includes meeting rooms where students can gather to discuss or work on projects together. The building also has two stages and a seminar room. A high school on the East Coast has included a literacy lab in its renovation, where students who need assistance with reading and writing can get help, much like college labs. An elementary school built a carpeted, recessed area for discussions and play-acting activities.

Clearly, spaces for the use of technologies are a must in this century. To start with, students need spaces where they can use computers to write, research, and perform many other academic tasks on a frequent basis. The Common Core State Standards, for example, require students to employ various media to examine a topic or issue. Schools and districts will need audio, visual, and computer technologies to address this standard in ways that match the workplace and college world. (See CCSS W 6, 8.)

Case Study #3: Resourcing Assignments

Not too long ago, while I was in a meeting with instructional coaches in a large urban district, it became clear that teachers did not have class sets of books to teach an Anchor assignment involving a character analysis, one of the standards the district had adopted. Without class sets, teachers would have to manage multiple, different titles, making teaching more difficult and time-consuming. As well, the books that were available were popular novels lacking the character development necessary for an analysis involving the role of conflict. Many of the novels we looked at had weak, stereotypical characters and trite story lines. To find appropriate texts, the coaches went online to find free short stories, a solution that ended up being used for other assignments as well (the Library of America and the Library of Congress are two examples of sites that offer free literature in print and visual formats). However, another impediment to teaching this assignment arose when students started their composing process. Schools had computer rooms, but it was hard for students to get in to use them, so the revision stage of the composing process didn't get the attention it should have. As a result, teachers and students had the time and capacity to do only one or two drafts. The lack of computer resources meant students couldn't work through multiple drafts and learn the skills involved in revising and editing.

Gathering resources that support reading, writing, and other literacy practices poses a challenge for districts committed to aligning subject-area curriculums to literacy standards, particularly the Common Core State Standards. A key element of the Common Core State Standards is "text complexity and the growth of comprehension" (CCSS, 2001, p. 8). To acquire skills necessary in college and careers, students need to learn how to access and read complex texts, both print and visual, that address a wide range of topics at various levels and involve challenging ideas in each core subject area. This is clearly a goal of the CCSS. Students need to learn to read electronic and printed texts in different formats for different purposes and to manage dense texts—those with complex sentences and transition words. Finding a variety of complex texts with the scope of topics and purposes stated in subject-area curriculums will demand collective thinking and resourcing, even new publications.

Reflection Activity: How do you define and think about "text complexity"? What resources would you need to provide a range of texts for students in topics relevant to your subject?

In the case just related, the teachers' attempts to teach Anchor assignments without class sets made their work harder but also less effective. Because students read a variety of titles instead of all reading the same title, it was impossible to address with any depth the finer points of the focus standards, such as analyzing a telling passage about a character. Having reading and visual resources is key to aligning coursework to the CCSS and some state standards; these standards specify types of texts and media, so teachers must have resources to address them. For example, CCSS RL7 directs 8th grade students to "analyze the extent to which a filmed or live production of a story or drama stays faithful to or departs from the text or script, evaluating the choices made by the director or actors." To teach RL7, teachers need access to appropriate films or must be able to take students to a live production. As well, this standard would require teachers to have knowledge of staging and directing in order to address the analysis. The bottom line is simple: To teach with fidelity and intentionality, no doubt teachers will need resources to make assignments matter.

Bolder Environments

To design "bolder" environments for teaching and learning is not necessarily about upsetting the apple cart. Small, strategic changes in practice can produce huge benefits in learning. In his discussion of the "talent code," Daniel Coyle (2009) says that a truly effective approach to education is one that involves "deep practice," the kind of teaching that fires circuits in the brain and ideas in the intellect (p. 209). The case studies described in this chapter have tried to show that reassessing your environment for the purpose of creating optimal conditions for assignments produces results, as well as engagement in learning. A strategic change may be a schedule that allows a vertical team of teachers to meet weekly or new spatial arrangements to encourage more fluid ways of interacting.

One small, bold move any teacher can make is to craft assignments that ask students to connect with the world outside of their classroom walls. Creating these assignments is increasingly necessary, not just a good idea, because students need to see that what they are learning has relevance to their present and future lives. Teaching assignments that connect students to the world outside the school is one of our best weapons against the apathy and boredom many students feel when confined to a classroom, where learning may seem irrelevant and tiresome. Just a few examples illustrate the possibilities:

- Students at a middle school cultivate a garden and cook meals and demonstrate the uses and benefits of local gardens to their community.
- In a border-town elementary school, students participate in a micro-society in which they hold court, run businesses, and manage payroll, among other institutional functions; they use the setting to teach new immigrants and younger students how to manage daily life, such as how to open a bank account.
- Students publish a book of essays that looks as professional as, well, a professional's book.
- Teachers across state borders blog about teaching a common assignment in which students "define" and "explain" a concept relevant to their subject.
- A group of future engineers write a manual for assembling a robot to compete in the regional robot games.
- Students cowrite with their teachers assignments for independent study. They examine issues of interest to them, interview community and national experts, and write and present their reports to a committee composed of educators and community members.
- Elementary school students write a proposal to local community-based organizations to raise funds for a trip to Washington, D.C., and research their trip on the Internet.
- Senior biology students participate as assistants alongside experts in a national research project.

Reflection Activity: How might you involve your students in assignments that relate to real-world experiences and situations?

Creating Environments for Ideas

Changing temporal and physical environments is a good way to make time and room for teaching and learning assignments, but the environment you create for ideas in curriculum design will ultimately make the most meaningful impact on achievement. Educators have learned from the small-school movement in the last two decades that just divvying up students into families or schools within a school doesn't change much about achievement if you don't use these environments to their advantage (Greene & Symonds, 2006). An eight-period day has the same effect on learning whether it's in a large or small school, and teaching literacy only in ELA classes won't increase the time and practice students receive in learning to read and communicate. Doing the same thing you've always done but in smaller units doesn't address the dynamics of the teaching and learning experience.

Schools that have implemented assignments have found that curriculum design also needs rethinking in ways that often affect the status quo, particularly if assignments challenge students in ways that take more time and thinking to accomplish. Three teachers in a Pennsylvania middle school came to that conclusion after noting a persistent trend in the school data: every year a group of graduating 8th graders were passed on despite grades of Ds and Fs. These students tended to be a year or more older than their peers and were likely to drop out of high school. Instead of merely tweaking the current curriculum and adding more tutoring time and other supports, the teachers decided on a curriculum design they called "Rapid Transit," a yearlong effort to provide students with an intensive literacy and math curriculum in a small-school environment. Their design strategy involved sequencing assignments and targeting literacy and math skills rather than starting with a scope and sequence based on content. In this design, content took second place to reading, writing, math, discourse, and academic behaviors. They identified the "biggest ideas" in social studies and science but did not make the long list of standards for those subjects the learning goal. As a result of Rapid Transit, most of the class progressed more than two years in their reading and math competencies, and a few gained more than four years. The class culminating assignment involved a short presentation to the school board on a school issue. Their appearance was a resounding success and received acknowledgment from the board for its thoughtfulness and presentation. These teachers' bold thinking and willingness to design a different learning environment and curriculum met the needs of students who had often been passed on without much attention to their minds and skills. Rapid Transit allowed them to reenter the mainstream curriculum in high school with a growing confidence in their ability to learn and to function in and out of school.

In the 1980s I was a member of a staff that designed the curriculum for a new public high school with a grant from the Panasonic Foundation. After a summer of meetings, we created a nongraded high school in which students moved through a three-year sequence of interdisciplinary courses as "families" of 9th, 10th, and 11th graders. The design planned for a senior year divided between off-campus and on-campus coursework and apprenticeships. Teams of four teachers taught two common sessions of 120 students a day. In this schedule, teachers prepared one plan for both sessions and an elective. This contrasted with the more common schedule in which we taught up to 180 students a day in six course periods each day.

We arrived at the nongraded design based on our knowledge of our students, many of whom were older and poorly prepared for high school. We wanted to create an environment that allowed us to address the academic and social needs of students who did not fit the official description of grade levels. We knew that age didn't have much to do with preparedness or ability and that our classes would already be mixed by age, with freshmen ranging from age 13 to 17. One of the deciding factors in our nongraded design was that no one really wanted to teach 9th graders corralled in classrooms by themselves—hormones and all. As an unintended result of our nongraded classrooms, discipline referrals dropped dramatically.

Our design, which we called "Gateways," was built to address the realities of teaching and learning in that community and to allow us to address students' needs while challenging their minds. Like the Rapid Transit curriculum design mentioned earlier, the goal was to accelerate learning as well as to challenge it, and we designed a curriculum that included assignments to ensure that students engaged in reading, writing, speaking, and listening throughout the day.

Reflection Activity: What would you do, if you could, to design an environment that makes teaching and learning engaging? Does the construction of the Core Curriculum State Standards in grade spans (4–5, 6–8, 9–10, 11–12) at some levels offer any opportunities to think differently?

Think Interdisciplinary

The Humanitas Curriculum in Los Angeles and the Gateways Curriculum in Santa Fe emerged in the 1980s from a tradition that views interdisciplinary curriculum as more powerful and effective than teaching curriculum in disciplinary silos. (Humanitas combines literature, philosophy, and history and is still practiced in some high schools in Los Angeles; see http://www .lausd.net/SLC_Schools/temps/garfield/ghs_humanitas_a.pdf.) More and more educators are designing schools so that students experience another kind of interdisciplinary education, one in which students participate in community life outside of the confines of the school or classroom. In Washington, D.C., students who attend School Without Walls meet in office buildings and museums to study and interact with professionals.

In Lancaster, Pennsylvania, in the late 1990s, the district established partnerships with the local hospital, rated one of the best in the region, and with the local technical and science college. Students who attended the hospital program graduated with an AA degree and a high school diploma, and more than one student received full-time employment at the hospital. The college partnered with the district because it needed students coming into its program to be better prepared in basic algebra. Students took the admissions exam, and when accepted, they attended algebra class with a high school instructor who coached them through the enrollment process and assisted them with the course and study habits. The project provided many students who would never have attended college otherwise to pursue higher education locally and elsewhere.

Make Environments Matter

The good news is that educators are designing environments that are innovative and exciting places for teachers and students. The New Technology High School in Napa, California, School Without Walls in Washington, D.C., and the Quest to Learn School in New York City exemplify such schools. Each has created intellectual and physical environments that encourage and motivate learners. In these schools, students learn "the basics" alongside knowledge and skills they need to participate in 21st-century society.

I encourage staff to engage in discussions to analyze the features at their schools that impede the teaching of assignments and encourage their professional communities to find solutions. It is a worthwhile endeavor—one that will make assignments matter.

◆ ◆ ◆ ◆ ◆

8

Assignments as Data

By considering multiple perspectives on available data, educators and policymakers can better judge whether efforts to lift today's students will produce the better educated citizenry our country needs.

—Rowan, Hall, & Haycock, 2010, p. 6

Assignments are rich sources of data about learning and teaching. These artifacts of classroom events tell useful narratives about the effectiveness of instructional choices and the progress students are making on reaching learning goals. Assignments should be read as an archaeologist reads artifacts, as data-stories in which pieces of the teaching and learning puzzle emerge if you read them closely and wisely. Research and well-documented accounts show that educators who consistently and intentionally use data to inform practice have a proven record for improving student progress (Chenoweth, 2007; Reeves, 2006; Rowan et al., 2010). Teachers have long practiced looking at student work to gauge student weaknesses and strengths and to determine progress in meeting learning goals. Student products also give feedback about the effectiveness of teacher work: how well assignments set the stage for instruction and how well that instruction taught the demands and qualities embedded in the assignments. Student products, particularly class sets, tell volumes about which strategies actually taught content or skills and which ones didn't take hold.

The purpose for collecting and analyzing assignments alongside student products is to provide feedback more than hard fact and to help teachers and administrators make choices about next steps, whether it's the next assignment or planning the next year's series of assignments. An analysis of an assignment and a class set of products might suggest, for example, eliminating some practices or reteaching content in a different way; or it might reveal, as in one school, the lack of resources that would have allowed a class of students to read the same novel.

This chapter describes a few ways to mine data from assignments and student products. One method helps you understand to what extent assignments are active in the larger curriculum and to what degree they embody the rigor of the CCSS or your state standards. Another focuses on the effectiveness of choices concerning the assignment and instructional strategies, and a third provides feedback on those supports that make teaching assignments possible. The final section discusses some solutions to the common questions data analyses raise about assignments and instruction. Ideally, you will go back and reread this book with a specific solution in mind.

Assignments as Classroom Artifacts

As a new teacher in the 1970s in San Francisco, I visited a school famous for its integrated arts program. Rhoda Kellogg, the founder and director, showed me the school's file room, where teachers kept copies of their lessons and student drawings collected several times over a year (you can view the collection at www.early-pictures.ch/kellogg/archive/en/). I clearly remember, these many decades later, how each student's collection she showed me told an evolving story not only of that student's abilities to produce artworks but of the child's unfolding maturation and understanding of aesthetic values. I could also see from the lesson plans that teachers had consistently built on sets of skills. This was my first professional lesson in the value of classroom artifacts in monitoring and tracking student learning. As data, these artworks, so neatly and carefully logged in those drawers, also showed me the impact a collection maintained over time can have on our understanding of developmental and academic progress.

Today we have resources to help us collect, examine, store, and monitor student progress and the effectiveness of instructional choices and resources. The two emerging CCSS assessment systems—PARCC and SBAC (see www.parcconline.org and www.k12.wa.us/SMARTER, respectively)—suggest frameworks in which formative and summative assessments, aided by computer-based systems, will monitor and record student learning frequently during a school year, providing a more robust collection of information about student progress than we have had nationally in the past. In a district or school, however, a well-planned series of assignments benchmarked by classroom assessments can also create a continuum of data-driven narratives about student progress.

Teachers at Tyler Elementary, which includes a PK–2 Spanish immersion program, wanted to know how well students could produce opinion-writing tasks (see CCSS K–5 W1). The writing students had done focused almost entirely around creative writing and activities, so the staff had no idea if these young students could manage academic modes and assignments. After a discussion about the differences between a "book report" and a "book review," the staff settled on a book review, in which students wrote about a book they recommended, or not, and stated why. Teachers started this cycle of instruction with an initial assessment, a book review writing prompt, to help them understand students' strengths and weaknesses and where they needed to focus instruction. They found that some students needed explicit instruction in practical skills, from penmanship to sentence construction, and all students, in the Spanish immersion program and the regular classes, needed instruction in the rhetoric of informed opinion appropriate for a book review. Although the older students had better practical skills, they also lacked skills in organizing an opinion/reasons structure in their reviews. The teachers gave the same prompt at the beginning of the year and at the end. During the year, they taught assignments focused on the rhetorical, language, and practical skills students needed to manage the year-end assessment prompt.

Teachers also taught skills related to forming an opinion and supporting it with evidence from a book. They employed a variety of strategies, oral and written, to help students gain better control over skills. As a result of this intentional teaching, students showed substantial progress—and not only on the classroom pre- and postassessments. The principal is confident that the use of these teacher-crafted assignments and assessments helped the school make large gains and meet its targets on the state assessment. This cycle of assessment-assignment-instruction-assessment is key to improving student learning because it creates a routine that allows for coherence and consistency (Marzano, 2007; Stiggins et al., 2006). The question is, however, To what extent are this cycle and its components functioning in your classrooms?

Calibrating Assignments: Data to Inform Practices and Curriculum Design

How many assignments, as defined in this book, do students engage in? Are they experiencing the same types of assignments? Are assignments relegated to one or two courses, or are they distributed among all courses? Are they aligned to grade-level standards? These are just some questions a staff might ask to help them track the frequency and type of assignments taught during a school term or year. To answer these data-driven questions requires a school staff to work together to collect samples over some time span—a few weeks, a semester, or even a year. Teachers contribute their assignments—or what they think are assignments—to a collection and analyze the collection to answer questions. Calibration is an engineering method of measuring against a standard, but you can use it to find out to what extent assignments are taught in your school or district and if they are, in fact, rigorous and challenging. Here is a process for conducting calibrations and the follow-up analyses:

- Decide on two or three questions to ask during an analysis and ask teachers to submit assignments relevant to the questions.
- Designate a safe location where teachers can drop off their assignments.

- Submit assignments with grade levels and subject indicated but without names of teachers or students. Use a code to identify submissions for record-keeping purposes.
- Create a data-collection template with questions for analysis. Use this as a professional development or team-meeting project.
- Create a calibration team consisting of teachers from the target disciplines and grades or across grades. You can also involve students, parents, and community members.
- Have a facilitator tally questions and hold a discussion around the results.

Calibrating the Frequency and Types of Tasks and Assignments

How much do you and your staff know about what kinds of tasks students are engaging in on a daily basis? To what degree are students engaged in assignments versus activities? A middle school that was facing a third year of low scores and low student achievement decided to collect all tasks—activities, assignments, and assessments—given over a month to students in all three grade levels. This collection amounted to more than 100 items, ranging from workbook dittos to lesson plans. A team outside of the school analyzed the collection and found only one assignment, from a science class. The vast majority of the tasks were textbook activities or fill-in-the-blank worksheets. When the staff reviewed the data, they were at first shocked, but over time they revamped their practices and included Anchor assignments. Eventually, assignments became part and parcel of the core curriculums. The result was that the school met its AYP and continued to demonstrate progress.

Reflection Activity: What narrative does this middle school collection tell about learning and teaching? What would you conclude about the connection between instruction and achievement?

Another way to cull data from assignments is to analyze class collections of student products resulting from an assignment. The best way to do this is to implement an Anchor assignment. When you analyze collections of products, you are looking for trends: Did all or most of the works address the prompt? Did all or most of the works show features delineated in the rubric? Where were the strengths? Where were the weaknesses? What does this tell about student progress?

Questions to ask:

- How many assignments were given this term? This semester? This year?
- How many tasks were activities?
- How many tasks were assessments?
- In what courses where assignments given, or not?
- How many assignments were given at home as homework rather than taught?
- What topics were covered? Were there redundancies?
- What did whole-class collections tell you about what instruction "took" and what did not or wasn't taught at all?
- What does this collection reveal about student progress?
- Did all or most of the works address the prompt?
- Did all or most of the works show features delineated in the rubric?
- Where were the strengths? Where were the weaknesses?
- What does this collection tell about student progress?

Calibrating Alignment to Standards

A superintendent of a small one-building district was stumped as to why her students weren't improving despite a number of designated high-impact programs purchased with Title I dollars operating in the schools. As a consultant to the district, I collected similar tasks from each grade as she visited classrooms, and I showed the superintendent a sample from each class. None of the papers had grade levels indicated on them. The superintendent could not tell which grade each paper came from as there was so little difference in demands: a 2nd grade paper looked like a 4th grade paper; and a 1st grade paper, like a 3rd grade paper. She couldn't tell the difference because all these samples asked students to write simple sentences without regard to linking or organizing thoughts. In other words, teaching stalled soon after students entered her school.

This exercise helped the superintendent literally see the lack of academic push in her curriculum and instruction. A theme that underscores this book is one that focuses on a close fit with meaningful demands and qualities, especially those expressed in standards. Calibrating assignments can reveal how tight that fit is and whether assignments align or fall short of the rigor stated in standards. This exercise in its various renditions can be done in a classroom, school, district, or state. South Carolina conducted a calibration to find out the degree to which tasks in schools were aligned with state standards. The collection revealed that tasks, including assignments, fell almost two or more years below grade level after 3rd grade (City, 2009). The state collected samples from 362 elementary and middle schools and 14 high schools. In both cases, assignments were deemed less rigorous than state standards. Clearly, the outcome of consistently lowering expectations in practices is low achievement.

You can perform your own calibration by again collecting tasks over a term or a semester. If teachers have an understanding of this book's definition of *assignment*, you might limit your collection to assignments. Follow these steps:

- Select one or more standards in the literacy area to calibrate.
- Create a collection.
- During a professional development session, post the standards on the wall and have teachers drop each task that aligns next to the corresponding standard. Tally how many align and how many do not.
- Form a study group to include teachers and, if desired, parents to assess the alignment against relevant standards.
- Create a data chart explaining alignment.

> **Reflection Activity:** Without calibrating, what is your estimate of how closely tasks and assignments align to the Common Core State Standards for a specified grade at your school? Compare that estimate to your research.

Questions to ask:

- Which standards are taught in assignments?
- How closely do assignments align to the CCSS, and which ones?
- Which standards were taught in each grade?
- Can you distinguish student work from a common assignment, such as a book report, from grade to grade?
- Are there redundancies among assignments in topic, product, or prompt?

Standards in Practice: Analyzing an Assignment and Products

In the 1990s a number of protocols were developed to analyze student work with a focus on determining weaknesses and strengths in student performances. It was rare, however, that those analyses looked at student work as evidence of the effectiveness of teacher work. A protocol developed by Ruth Mitchell (1996) involves teachers and administrators in an effort to track the effectiveness of a single task and its impact on student learning. *Standards in Practice* (SIP) is a protocol involving a group of teachers who work through a process of analysis of one teacher's task. They analyze the task to determine if it is aligned to standards and sets appropriate expectations for performance. Teachers score the class set of products and tally their scores. At the end of the process, the group settles on next steps to improve practice and their assignments. Staff from the Education Trust have coached schools and districts around the country for 20 years in SIP. As a data-collection method, SIP can also provide feedback about the quality of assignments as well as student progress on sets of standards. It also provides excellent professional development because each step involves teacher thinking, problem solving, and collaboration on what matters most in the classroom—student learning.

Questions to ask:

- Are the assignment prompt and rubric aligned to CCSS or other standards?
- Is the product appropriate to the age and grade level?
- Is the instructional plan sufficiently detailed with appropriate strategies?
- Does the student work indicate that the assignment was successful? If not, why not?
- Does the assignment merit the time and effort involved in teaching and learning?

Collecting Data About Supports for Teaching Assignments

Teaching assignments is intensive work, requiring time and effort. You can collect feedback on the circumstances and conditions that affect teaching assignments in your environments in order to create more supportive schedules, spaces, and resources. Studies have shown that workplace conditions greatly affect how teachers react to their schools and their satisfaction with their jobs. In a policy report by the Center for Teaching Quality, the authors cite studies that show that

> successful efforts to raise teaching quality and student achievement, especially in high-needs schools, require *an intensive focus on working conditions*: making sure teachers teach in the fields in which they are prepared; have adequate time to work with colleagues on matters of instruction; have ready access to information, materials and technology; and receive helpful feedback about their teaching. (Berry, Daughtrey, & Wieder, 2009, p. 6)

Since effectively teaching assignments depends in large part on these factors, it is worth a staff's efforts to find out what conditions might impede teaching assignments.

Here are some common tools and methods you can use to collect data and feedback on environments:

- Conduct surveys around specific questions about time, resources, and spaces.
- Conduct focus groups around the relationship between assignments and environments.
- Write assignments that collect data about those same assignments and involve students in the research by documenting the amount of time they spend on an assignment and its elements: e.g., How much time did it take you to find research articles? How much time did it take you to create an outline?
- Compare your data with a partner school that involves students in assignment-rich coursework, such as AP or IB courses.
- Compare your data to a local college's freshman English or history course.

Reflection Activity: How might you collect data and feedback on the conditions in your school that affect when and how assignments are taught? What do you expect to find? Did the results match your notions?

Questions to ask:

- Is the curriculum crowded with "must dos" that do not allow for extended time on assignments?
- Do teachers have schedules that allow for collaboration to score and to coteach?
- Is it explicit or implicit that core and other teachers share responsibilities for teaching and assessing student progress in literacy and math?

- Are teachers encouraged to experiment and try more challenging assignments?
- Does professional development focus on skills needed to teach assignments, including crafting good prompts and instructional plans?
- Are ESL and special education teachers also involved in teaching assignments, and do they participate in professional development?

An analysis can help you gauge how much and in what way you might increase demands in the next assignment. For example, in the book review assignment described earlier, the students have not grasped the difference between retelling and supporting an opinion with reasons. Teachers would probably choose to reteach what an opinion is, a variety of ways to express one, and how to develop a set of reasons in an opinion work.

Common Problems and Some Solutions

Over the years, I've collected a list of problems that have emerged from data culled from analyzing assignments and products. Here are the top five problems, with some brief suggestions for solutions.

Problem #1: Assignments lack rigor and challenge.
Solutions:

- Cocraft assignments in vertical teams, from grade to grade, particularly at the transition points, such as 5th to 6th, 8th to 9th, or 12th to postsecondary.
- Borrow proven assignment prompts from Advanced Placement, LDC, state assessments, and other sources.
- Rewrite standards as prompts.
- Teach, revise, analyze, and reteach until you get it right.
- Ask students and parents or caregivers to give you feedback.

Problem #2: There's not enough time.
Solutions:

- Conduct a time analysis around teaching tasks, scoring, and other factors.
- Rework schedules so that teachers have time to collaborate.
- Rework schedules so that teachers can coteach over two or more periods.
- Conduct an analysis of "time on assignments" to better understand where time is most needed. For example, students may need more time to revise drafts.
- Shorten and streamline your assignments so that they don't drag on.
- Reduce the number of focus standards so that you can emphasize two or three critical skills and content topics at a time.

Problem #3: Assignments are not taught explicitly enough.
Solutions:

- Survey teachers to find out what skills they need to teach components of an assignment's instruction. For example, teachers may need to gain skills in teaching logic or note-taking.
- Analyze homework to see if it is replacing classroom teaching.
- Provide time to collaborate on assignments and share expertise.
- Pair teachers to teach an assignment, for example, an English and biology teacher on an essay about cells.
- Record on video specific strategies being taught, such as a seminar on selecting credible and appropriate citations.
- Create a list of online professional development resources.

Problem #4: Assignments aren't really assignments.
Solutions:

- Rewrite activities as assignments.
- Borrow well-crafted and proven prompts.

- Assign common assignments to a grade or discipline.
- Insert assignments in projects and units.

Problem #5: Students don't want to do assignments.
Solutions:

- Vary assignments by topic, skill sets, and products.
- Include authentic activities and connect students to the world outside of school.
- Make some form of discussion an instructional mainstay, because young people love to talk.
- Ask students to write their own assignments.
- Create journals, videos, or other formats in which students can display their good products to others, in and out of school.

A Powerful Solution: Reteaching

While waiting for a flight, I saw a greeting card in an airport shop with the saying, "Education is achievement." It seemed to me that there was wisdom in that college graduation card that can be applied to making assignments matter, because collecting data and analyzing classroom artifacts, particularly assignments and student products, is a search for solutions that lead to achievement. When in doubt about what to do next, the simple act of reteaching is a powerful solution in response to feedback about assignments and their effectiveness in the teaching and learning cycle. Students—all students—always need more practice or additional instruction on some set of skills or content. When reteaching, teachers also get a chance to retry—or eliminate, perhaps—instructional strategies. *Reteaching is not just doing the same assignment again.* Rather, it should simultaneously repair and ratchet up demands, gently but firmly moving students along a learning progression toward achievement.

Sometimes data tell us we need a new approach or strategies to support assignments. If so, think about employing strategies you have read about in this book, or search out effective practices elsewhere. Maybe a seminar would help students better understand abstract concepts, for example, or perhaps a 15-minute lecture would do. Teachers can reteach without boring a class with "the same ol' thing." As when spiraling a series of assignments, teachers can reteach some skills and content while adding new ones. Reteaching is responsive teaching because it ensures students reach learning goals even if it requires another try.

The decision about what to reteach starts with an analysis of a class set of student products created during a previous assignment to determine the extent to which students have learned the assignment's content and skills. A class set is necessary because you will see trends of what was and wasn't learned in the collective works. For example, you might see that students didn't cite resources at all or didn't manage to include sufficient supporting details. You determine where students may need more direct instruction or less intervention.

Reflection Activity: Look at the following 5th grade student sample, indicative of a class set. What would you reteach? Would you add a new skill? Use the CCSS 5th grade W1 to help you decide.

Dear Eleanor,

I'm enjoying being back in school because it's fun to see my friends all in one place. I have a new teacher this year, and it looks like we are going to learn a lot of new things. Thank you for your letter. I enjoyed hearing about your new puppy and Charro is a good name for a pet. I just finished the book *Dragonwings* by Laurence Yep. The book starts in China the year 1903 when a boy named Moon Shadow goes to live with his father Windrider in San Francisco California. Laurence Yep tells a really good story about how the characters Moon Shadow and Windrider work together on a flying machine. When they need help from each other they would help each other instead of saying no.

Sincerely,
Michael

✦ ✦ ✦ ✦ ✦

A well-crafted assignment, well taught, is the hallmark of the profession. This book strives to give teachers guidance in their efforts to deliver quality instruction to students every day in their classrooms. As well, it aims to guide administrators and other educators in their efforts to support teachers by creating the professional environments and policies that make teaching and learning assignments possible.

I end this book by invoking Frances Wright once more, who in a commencement in 1852 reminds us that "it will appear evident upon attentive consideration that equality of intellectual and physical advantages is the only sure foundation of liberty, and that such equality may best, and perhaps only, be obtained by a union of interests and cooperation in labor."

Part 4

Appendixes

Appendix A

Assignment Planning Guide

Steps		Your Assignment: _____
1	Identify content, focus standards, and skills.	
2	Determine a product.	
3	Identify demands and qualities.	
4	Write a prompt.	
5	Write a rubric.	
6	Do your assignment.	
7	Make an instructional plan.	

Appendix B

Unit Plan

Use this template to construct a course by adding units in sequence.

Unit Theme & Content:

Unit Time Line:

Products: (e.g., 1 essay, 1 timeline, 1 speech, etc.)

Focus Standards:

Assignment(s): (Write prompt and rubric)

Assessment(s):

Appendix C

Glossary

Activity—a task that is not scored or graded but is used to help students acquire and practice content and skills. Examples include a wide range of strategies, such as a value line, pair-sharing, and literature circles.

Alignment—the degree to which an assignment or other tasks confer with curriculum standards. Assignments are "aligned" when they involve demands stated in curriculum standards.

Assessment—a task given to students independent of instruction to monitor their understanding of content or use of a skill set and scored against a rubric. *Assignments Matter* makes a clear distinction between taught tasks and those that are not.

Assignment—a task charging students to engage in content and skills distinguished by a prompt, a product, and a rubric; an assignment is intentionally taught and focused on student achievement.

Course—a scope and sequence that creates a coherent presentation of some aspect of a discipline and is organized around units of study involving assignments and other tasks.

Demands—charges to do something with texts, content, and skills; for example, "read three texts on cell formation" or "write an opinion."

Instructional plan—documentation of a series of instructional events that lead to the completion of an assignment's product.

Instructional strategy—an activity used to teach a skill or to develop understanding of content.

Qualities—descriptors that modify demands, as in "read closely" or "cite accurately." Rubrics communicate the qualities that should be evident in student products.

Rigor—the confluence of demands and qualities often informed by curriculum standards or other learning goals. High rigor is characterized by grade-level academic challenge that includes complex demands and qualities. Low rigor is characterized by simplistic demands and tends to align to standards below a grade level.

Rubric—a qualifying statement(s) that describes expectations for performances and products based on standards and assignment demands. Rubrics come in a variety of formats, including analytical and holistic, one-level and multilevel.

Task—an instructional event or undertaking in order to teach content and skills. Assignments, assessments, and activities are all tasks.

Appendix D

Sample Assignment Prompts

Prompts Vertically Aligned to the CCSS RL7

Elementary school: Give an oral presentation in which you make connections between the movie *Wind in the Willows* and the original story by Kenneth Grahame. Point out three instances where the movie version follows the fairy tale. (RL4.7)

Middle school: Read Raymond Carver's story "Everything Must Go" and view the movie starring Will Ferrell. Write a movie review in which you analyze the extent to which the film stays faithful to or departs from the story, evaluating the choices made by the director. (RL8.7)

High school: Write an essay in which you analyze multiple interpretations of the classic theme of revenge and its repercussions prominent in Greek tragedy, evaluating how each version interprets the source text. Include at least one play by Shakespeare and one play by an American dramatist. (RL11–12.7)

Sample Performance Tasks from the CCSS Appendix B (Note: These are not yet prompts but can be crafted as prompts, as above.)

Students *compare and contrast a firsthand account* of African American ballplayers in the Negro Leagues *to a secondhand account* of their treatment found in books such as Kadir Nelson's *We Are the Ship: The Story of Negro League Baseball*, attending to the *focus* of each account *and the information provided* by each. (RI4.6)

Students *explain how* Sandra Cisneros's choice of words *develops the point of view* of *the young speaker* in her story "Eleven." (RL6.6)

Students *analyze how* the *character* of Odysseus from Homer's *Odyssey*—a "man of twists and turns"—reflects *conflicting motivations* through his *interactions with other characters* in the epic poem. They articulate how his conflicting loyalties during his long and complicated journey home from the Trojan War both *advance the plot* of Homer's epic and *develop themes*. (RL9–10.3)

Literacy Design Collaborative Sample Prompts for Template Task 2

The template task collection is available at www.literacydesigncollaborative. org.

Middle School

Background: Kurt Vonnegut Jr. creates an interesting social environment in his short story "Harrison Bergeron," in which all people are made equal by the government. In this module, you are to consider an interesting question raised in the story about this utopian world and argue for or against the world that is created in Vonnegut's story "Harrison Bergeron."

Prompt: Does Vonnegut consider "equality" a viable social condition? After reading "Harrison Bergeron," write an essay that addresses the question and support your position with evidence from the text.

Extension: Create a multimedia presentation drawn from your essay in which you describe a utopian society for a presentation on community night.

High School

Background: Every society operates with a mixed economic system, combining the influences of market and command models in order to form a functioning economy and government. Individual countries have unique combinations of the market and command influences, depending on how countries prioritize different economic goals. Students will engage in activities and take notes on the content for three days before beginning the module. Students will also keep all work in a portfolio.

Prompt: What combination of market and command systems do you believe creates an ideal mixed economy? After reading informational and opinion texts, write an essay that addresses the question and supports your position with evidence from the texts. Be sure to acknowledge competing views.

Extension (optional): Students invite local experts to participate in a formal class debate about the future of America's economic system using their essays and other research to defend their market and command preferences on different topics (health care, welfare, education, taxes, etc.).

Prompts Adapted from the Partnership for 21st Century Skills
www.21centuryskills.org

Critical Thinking and Problem Solving
Grade 4: Using photographs from the Library of Congress and letters from the National Archives, examine in a report social injustices present in our society in the period from 1890 to 1920 and the ways in which Jane Addams takes social action.

Grade 8: How much schooling do you need to get the kind of job you would like to have? After researching salaries and education/training requirements of three careers of your choice, create a chart comparing each choice.

Grade 12: Analyze an article for your student newspaper from the satiric website www.theonion.com. Identify the elements of satire used in an article in a critique, evaluating the effectiveness of the piece as a commentary on current events.

Sample Prompts from the PARCC and SBAC Frameworks

PARCC (CCSS Match 11–12.RI.8)
www.parcconline.org

Delineate and evaluate the argument that Thomas Paine makes in *Common Sense*. Assess the reasoning present in his analysis, including the premises and purposes of his essay.

SBAC (CCSS Match: W4.4 and L4.4)
www.k12.wa.us/SMARTER/

Scientists like to study animals in their natural habitat. That means that a shark scientist has to study sharks in the oceans where they live. Shark scientists are scuba divers who go deep into the ocean to learn more about sharks.

Read and discuss "Facts About Sharks" by Susanna Batchelor. *Think about how these two types of sharks are the same and also how they are different.* <u>*Which shark would you study if you were a shark scientist, and why?*</u>

1. Decide which shark you would want to study if you were a scientist.

2. Find the best shark facts to support your reasons.

3. Explain your reasons. Be sure to use facts about hammerhead sharks and whale sharks to explain why you would study the shark you chose and not study the other shark.

You can use a graphic organizer to help you plan your writing. Remember to <u>pick the best facts</u> to support your opinion, and not every detail you can find. You must <u>explain how the facts support your opinion and each of your reasons.</u>

Sample Advanced Placement Prompts
http://apcentral.collegeboard.com/apc/public/courses/teachers_
corner/3501.html

2011 Form B

In *The Writing of Fiction* (1925), novelist Edith Wharton states the
following:

*At every stage in the progress of his tale the novelist must rely on what may be
called the illuminating incident to reveal and emphasize the inner meaning of
each situation. Illuminating incidents are the magic casements of fiction, its
vistas on infinity.*

Choose a novel or play that you have studied and write a well-organized
essay in which you describe an "illuminating" episode or moment and
explain how it functions as a "casement," a window that opens onto the
meaning of the work as a whole. Avoid mere plot summary.

FRQs U.S. History 2003

Analyze the responses of Franklin D. Roosevelt's administration to the
problems of the Great Depression. How effective were these responses?
How did they change the role of the federal government? Use the documents and your knowledge of the period 1929–1941 to construct your
essay.

Prompt from a Spanish Immersion Elementary PK–2 Program

¿Cual es tu parte favorita del cuento "El niño de pan de jengibre"? (CCSS
W1)

Appendix E

Resources

These are just a few of the web-based resources where you can find topics and lessons to adapt as assignments and units.

Advanced Placement—http://apcentral.collegeboard.com/apc/public/courses/teachers_corner/3501.html

Core Knowledge— http://coreknowledge.org

Library of Congress—http://catalog.loc.gov/

One World Education—www.oneworldeducation.org

PARCC—www.parcconline.org

PBS—www.thirteen.org/edonline

Read Write Think (NCTE)—www.readwritethink.org

SBAC—www.k12.wa.us/SMARTER/

Smithsonian Institute—www.smithsonianeducation.org

21st Century Partnership—www.21stcenturyskills.org

U.S. Census Bureau—www.census.gov/mso/www/educate/resource.htm

References

ACT. (2006). *Reading between the lines: What the ACT reveals about college and career readiness in reading.* Iowa City, IA: ACT.

Ausubel, D. (1963). *The psychology of meaningful verbal learning.* New York: Grune and Stratton.

Barth, P. A., & Dougherty, E. (1997, April 2). How to close the achievement gap. *Education Week.*

Berry, B., Daughtrey, A., & Wieder, A. (2009, November). Teaching effectiveness and the conditions that matter most in high-needs schools: A policy brief. Retrieved April 24, 2012, from http://www.teachingquality.org/sites/default/files/Tch_effective_twc_final.pdf

Berry, B., et al. (2011). *Teaching 2030: What we must do for our students and our public schools . . . Now and in the future.* New York: Teachers College Press.

Briars, D. J. (2011, January). Tools and strategies for considering instructional materials for implementing the CCSS. Retrieved April 24, 2012, from http://www.lsri.uic.edu/ccss/ccss_bo_briars.pdf

Caperton, G. (2006, April 7). *Advanced Placement program: Connecting students to college success.* Paper presented to the Commission for the Future of Higher Education.

Chall, J. S. (2000). *The academic achievement challenge: What really works in the classroom.* New York: Guilford Press.

Chenoweth, K. (2007). *"It's being done": Academic success in unexpected schools.* Cambridge, MA: Harvard Education Press.

Cioran, E. (2001). Retrieved April 24, 2012, from http://www.brainyquote.com/quotes/quotes/e/emilemcio181757.html

City, E. (2009, August). Instructional rounds [PowerPoint presentation]. Beaverton, OR.

City, E., Elmore, R., Fieman, S., & Teitel, L. (2009). *Instructional rounds in education: A network approach to improving teaching and learning.* Cambridge, MA: Harvard Education Press.

Common Core State Standards for English Language Arts. (2001). Retrieved April 24, 2012, from http://www.corestandards.org/the-standards/english-language-arts-standards

Conley, D. T. (2005). *College knowledge: What it really takes for students to succeed and what we can do about it.* San Francisco: Jossey-Bass.

Conley, D. T. (2011). *Designing common assessments to be measures of college and career readiness.* Retrieved April 24, 2012, from https://www.epiconline.org/files/pdf/DesigningCommonAssessments_2011.pdf

Coyle, D. (2009). *The talent code.* New York: Bantam Press.

Crawford, M., & Dougherty, E. (2004). *Updraft/downdraft: Secondary education in the crosswinds of reform.* Lanham, MD: Rowman and Littlefield.

Crawford, M., Galiatsos, S., & Lewis, A.C. (2011). *The 1.0 guidebook to LDC: Linking secondary school core content to the common core state standards.* Retrieved April 24, 2012, from http://www.literacydesigncollaborative.org/

Danielson, C. (1996). *Enhancing professional practice: A framework for teaching.* Alexandria, VA: ASCD.

Education Trust. (2005, November). *Gaining traction, gaining ground: How some high schools accelerate learning for struggling students.* Washington, DC: Education Trust. Available: http://www.edtrust.org

Education Trust. (2006, Summer). *Standards in practice: Using data to organize for success.* Washington, DC: Education Trust.

Education Trust. (2008, October). Counting on graduation: An agenda for state leadership. Available: http://www.edtrust.org

Elmore, R. (2010). Leading an instructional core: An interview with Richard Elmore. *In Conversation, 11*(3), 1–12. Retrieved April 24, 2012, from http://www.edu.gov.on.ca/eng/policyfunding/leadership/Summer2010.pdf

Fairtest. (2007, August 27). The value of formative assessment. Retrieved April 24, 2012, from http://fairtest.org/value-formative-assessment-pdf

Fiello, D. T. (2005). *Aligning instruction to California fifth-grade English language arts content standards* (dissertation). Pepperdine University, Los Angeles, CA. Retrieved April 24, 2012, from http://gradworks.umi.com/31/91/3191651.html

Fullan, M. (2007). *The new meaning of educational change* (4th ed.). New York: Teachers College Press.

Goe, L. (2009). Key issues: Using value-added models to identify and support highly effective teachers. *Tips and Tools Document.* Retrieved April 24, 2012, from http://www.tqsource.org

Greene, J., & Symonds, W. C. (2006, June 26). Bill Gates gets schooled. *Business Week.* Retrieved April 24, 2012, from http://www.businessweek.com/print/magazine/content/06_26/b3990001.htm?chan=gl

Hattie, J. (2008). *Visible learning: A synthesis of over 800 meta-analyses relating to achievement.* New York: Routledge Press.

Herman, J. L., Osmundson, E., & Deitel, R. (2010). Benchmark assessment for improved learning. Retrieved April 24, 2012, from http://www.aacompcenter.org/cs/aacc/download/rs/25400/R2_benchmark_report_Herman.indd.pdf?x-r=pcfile_d

Hunter, M. (1993). *Enhancing teaching.* New York: Macmillan.

Joint Information System Committee. (2006). *Designing space for effective learning: A guide to 21st century learning space design.* Retrieved April 24, 2012, from http://www.jisc.ac.uk/uploaded_documents/JISClearningspaces.pdf

Jupp, B. (2009). *What states can do to improve teacher effectiveness.* Washington, DC: The Education Trust.

Marzano, R. J. (2003). *What works in schools: Translating research into action.* Alexandria, VA: ASCD.

Marzano, R. J. (2007). *Art and science of teaching: A comprehensive framework for effective instruction.* Alexandria, VA: ASCD.

Matsumura, L. C. (2005). *Creating high-quality classroom assignments.* Lanham, MD: Scarecrow Press.

Mitchell, R. (1996). *Front-end alignment: Using standards to steer educational change.* Golden, CO: Fulcrum Press.

National Education Commission on Time and Learning. (1994). *Prisoners of time.* Washington, DC: U.S. Department of Education.

Noble, J., & Sawyer, R. (2004, Spring). Is high school GPA better than admission test scores for predicting academic success in college? *College and University, 79*(4), 17–22.

Pink, D. (2009). *Drive: The surprising truth about what motivates us.* New York: Riverhead Press.

Reeves, D. (2006). *The learning leader.* Alexandria, VA: ASCD.

Research for Action. (2011, June). *Establishing a strong foundation: District and school supports for classroom implementation of the LDC framework.* Paper presented at the Unleashing Group Genius Gates Foundation Partners Conference, New Orleans, LA.

Richtel, M. (2011, February 3). In classroom of the future, stagnant scores. *New York Times.*

Roberts, T., & Billings, L. (2012). *Teaching critical thinking: Using seminars for 21st century learning.* Larchmont, NY: Eye on Education.

Roberts, T., & Billings, L. (1998). *Teaching for understanding: the Paideia classroom.* Larchmont, NY: Eye on Education.

Rose, D. (n.d.). What is UDL? The role of technology in UDL, the importance of technology. Research and advisors: Webinar series. Retrieved April 24, 2012, from http:// teacher.scholastic.com/products/ReadAbout/research/webinars_rose.htm

Rowan, A., Hall, D., & Haycock, K. (2010, January). Gauging the gaps: A deeper look at student achievement. Retrieved April 24, 2012, from http://www.edtrust.org/sites/ edtrust.org/files/publications/files/NAEP Gap_0.pdf

Sanders, W. T., & Rivers, R. T. (1996). *Cumulative and residual effects of teachers on future student academic achievement.* Knoxville, TN: University of Tennessee Value-Added Research and Assessment Center. Retrieved April 24, 2012, from http://www.cgp. upenn.edu/pdf/Sanders_Rivers-TVASS_teacher%20effects.pdf

Schmidt, W. H., McKnight, C. C., Cogan, L.S., Jakewerth, P. M., & Houng, R. T. (1999). *Facing the consequences: Using TIMSS for a close look at U.S. mathematics and science education.* Norwell, MA: Kluwer Academic Publishers.

Schmoker, M. (2006). *Results now: How we can achieve unprecedented improvements in teaching and learning.* Alexandria, VA: ASCD.

Schmoker, M. (2011). *Focus: Elevating the essentials to radically improve student learning.* Alexandria, VA: ASCD.

SEDL. (1997). Professional communities: What are they and why are they important? Available: http://www.sedl.org/change/issues/issues61.html

Sharratt, L., & Fullan, M. (2012). *Putting FACES on the data: What great leaders do!* Thousand Oaks, CA: Corwin.

Sparks, S. D. (2011, April 26). Studies find "desirable difficulties" help students learn. *Education Week.* Retrieved April 24, 2012, from http://www.edweek.org/ew/articles/2011/04/27/29stability-2.h30.html

Stein, M. K., Brown, C. A., & Forman, E. (1996). Instructional tasks and the development of student capacity to think and reason. *Educational Research and Evaluation, 2*(1), 50–80.

Stein, M. K., Smith, M. S., Henningsen, M. A., & Silver, E. (2000). *Implementing standards-based mathematics instruction.* New York: Teachers College Press.

Stiggins, R. J., Aster, J. A., Chappius, J., & Chappius, S. (2006). *Classroom assessment for student learning: Doing it right, using it well.* Boston: Allyn & Bacon.

U.S. Department of Education. (2002–2009). What works clearinghouse. Retrieved April 24, 2012, from http://ies.ed.gov/ncee/wwc

Wright, F. (1829). *Course of popular lectures.* Retrieved April 24, 2012, from http://www.spartacus.schoolnet.co.uk/REwright.htm

Wright, F. (1852, January 26). Explanatory notes, respecting the nature and objects of the institution of Nashoba, and of the principles upon which it was founded. Addressed to the friends of human improvement, in all countries and all nations. *The Correspondent, 93.*

Wurtzel, J. (2007, Fall). The professional, personified: Districts find results by combining a vision of professionalism with common tasks and goals. *Journal of Staff Development, 28*(4), 30–35.

Zeiderman, H. (1984). *A guide for leading discussions using touchstones, Vol. I.* Annapolis, MD: CSM Press.

Index

Note: The letter *f* following a page number denotes a figure.

◆ ◆ ◆ ◆ ◆

About the Author

Eleanor Dougherty is a consultant with education foundations and agencies on curriculum and professional development. During her career, she has taught in public, private, and postsecondary institutions and worked in both practice and policy organizations, including the U.S. Department of Education and the Education Trust. She has participated in grants from the Gates Foundation and the Panasonic Foundation and has assisted districts and organizations with diverse student populations across the country.

Her work over the last two decades has focused on literacy and its role in the larger curriculum, particularly in the core subjects. Dougherty is currently involved in developing a national literacy strategy, *Literacy Design Collaborative,* to help teachers in the core subjects align their practice to the Common Core State Standards. She is the author of two previous books and articles addressing the challenge of transforming standards into practice.

Related ASCD Resources: Common Core State Standards

At the time of publication, the following ASCD resources were available (ASCD stock numbers appear in parentheses). For up-to-date information about ASCD resources, go to www.ascd.org. You can search the complete archives of *Educational Leadership* at http://www.ascd.org/el.

ASCD EDge Group

Exchange ideas and connect with other educators interested in Common Core State Standards on the social networking site ASCD EDge™ at http://ascdedge.ascd.org/.

Online Courses

Common Core and Literacy Strategies: English Language Arts (#PD11OC135)
Crafting Curriculum: Using Standards (#PD09OC25)

Books

The Core Six: Essential Strategies for Achieving Excellence with the Common Core by Silver Strong & Associates (#113007)
Understanding Common Core State Standards by John Kendall (#112011)
Making Standards Useful in the Classroom by Robert J. Marzano and Mark W. Haystead (#108006)
From Standards to Success: A Guide for School Leaders by Mark R. O'Shea (#105017)

DVDs

Unpacking the Common Core Standards Using the UbD Framework with Jay McTighe and Grant Wiggins (#612059)

THE WHOLE CHILD The Whole Child Initiative helps schools and communities create learning environments that allow students to be healthy, safe, engaged, supported, and challenged. To learn more about other books and resources that relate to the whole child, visit www.wholechildeducation.org.

For more information: send e-mail to member@ascd.org; call 1-800-933-2723 or 703-578-9600, press 2; send a fax to 703-575-5400; or write to Information Services, ASCD, 1703 N. Beauregard St., Alexandria, VA 22311-1714 USA.